JIMMY DEAN
on
JIMMY DEAN

JIMMY
DEAN
ON
JIMMY
DEAN

Consultant: Joseph Humphreys

Plexus, London

Jimmy Dean on Jimmy Dean
  1. Cinema films. Acting. Dean, James, 1931
  Biographies
  791.43′028′0924

  ISBN 0-85965-126-6

Phototypeset by St. George Typesetting, Redruth
Printed in Great Britain by The Bath Press, Avon

Acknowledgements

We would like to thank Joseph Humphreys for drawing on his
extensive knowledge of James Dean's life and career in the
compilation of this book, and for providing rare photographs,
magazines and memorabilia from his personal James Dean
archive.

 Our thanks also go to Helen Gummer and John Howlett for
their research, and to Mary Davies for sifting through masses of
material for us.

 We would also like to thank the following individuals and
organisations who contributed to the gathering of pictures for
this book: Ray Connolly for the use of material from his film
Jimmy Dean: The First American Teenager, Joseph Humphreys,
Sanford Roth, Roy Schatt, Phil Stern, Dennis Stock/Magnum
Photos, the British Film Institute, IPC and Warner Brothers.

 In our research we have referred to the following books and
we extend our grateful thanks to the authors: *James Dean* by
John Howlett, *James Dean: the Mutant King* by David Dalton,
James Dean: The American Icon by David Dalton, *I, James Dean* by
T T Thomas, *The Death of James Dean* by Warren Newton Beath,
James Dean: A Short Life by Venable Herndon, *The James Dean
Story* by Ronald Martinetti, *James Dean Story* by René Chateau,
Giant by Edna Ferber, *The Immortal* by Walter Ross, *James Dean:
A Biography* by William Bast, *James Dean Is Not Dead* by Stephen
Morrissey, *James Dean ou Le Mal de Vivre* by Yves Salgues, *James
Dean Revisited* by Dennis Stock, *James Dean: A Portrait* by Roy
Schatt, *The Real James Dean Story* by John Gilmore, *Rebel* by
Royston Ellis, *Wish You Were Here, Jimmy Dean*.

 We must also thank the following magazines and publications
which have been of invaluable help in the compilation of the
book: *16 Magazine, Brigitte, Cinémonde, Fans' Star Library: The Late
James Dean, James Dean Album, James Dean Anniversary Book,
Jimmy Dean Returns, Illustrated, Life, Look, Modern Screen, Movie
Spotlight, New Film Star Annual, Photoplay, Picturegoer,
Pictureshow, The Real James Dean Story, Top Spot*.

 It has not been possible in all cases to trace the copyright
sources, and the publishers would be glad to hear from any
such unacknowledged copyright holders.

Contents

Chapter 1

CHILDHOOD

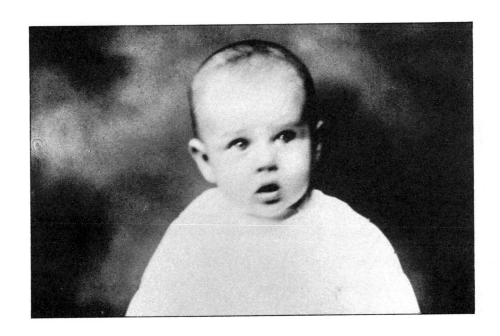

'Having no mother is tough on a kid,
you know.' Jimmy Dean

'My life story seems so dull to me that I can't really tell it right without the "Funeral March" or "Hearts And Flowers" providing a mournful background.' – *Jimmy Dean*

James Byron Dean was born on 8 February 1931 in the small town of Marion, Indiana. His father, Winton Dean, was a respectable dental technician who worked for the Federal Government, but it was his more artistic mother, Mildred, who was to become the dominant influence on Jimmy in those early years.

'My mother named me after Lord Byron.' – *Jimmy Dean*

'James Byron is all I have in the world, and God knows I'm all he has.' – *Mildred Dean*

On the early tensions in the relationship with his father and the happy times with his mother:

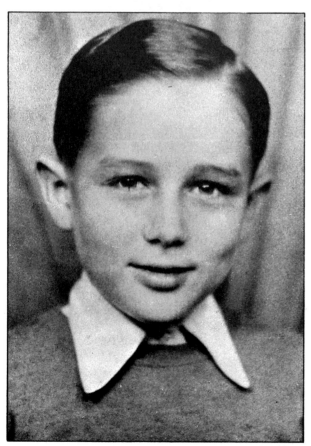

'I never understood him. I never understood what he was after, what sort of person he'd been, because he never tried to get on my side of the fence, or to try and see things the way I saw them when I was little. I was always with Mom and we were very close. She used to turn things in the water, and then she would make the water turn like a whirlpool by turning her finger around and around the boat...It used to make me dizzy! I'd laugh and laugh and I wanted to do it myself, but what happened was that I would start turning the water around and the boat would flop over upside down and it'd sink. I never understood it - how she could keep it from sinking.' – *Jimmy Dean*

Such happy times were carefully stored away in Jimmy's memory, and were never forgotten.
'An old album of pictures I'm carrying around in my head.' – *Jimmy Dean*

When Jimmy was four years old the Dean family moved west to Santa Monica, California, and Jimmy was enrolled at the Brentwood School. There he suffered from the stigma of being an outsider and made few friends.
'Everything is so artificial here. I want my son to grow up where things are real and simple.' – *Mildred Dean*

On being liked:
'One of the deepest drives of human nature is the desire to be appreciated, the longing to be liked, to be held in esteem, to be a sought-after person.' – *Jimmy Dean*

'He had a large anxiety to do many different things. He had to try everything and he soon outgrew most of the toys we bought him. He always seemed to be getting ahead of himself.' – *Winton Dean*

In 1939, Jimmy's mother was diagnosed as having breast cancer, and her health deteriorated rapidly. Soon she was admitted to hospital. Winton tried to explain that she was going to die.

Below left: Jimmy aged 9. Below: A rare photograph of Jimmy with his parents, Mildred and Winton. Below right: Jimmy with a playmate called Mary Lou.
Bottom: 'Top Spot' ran a pictorial biography of Dean in 1959.

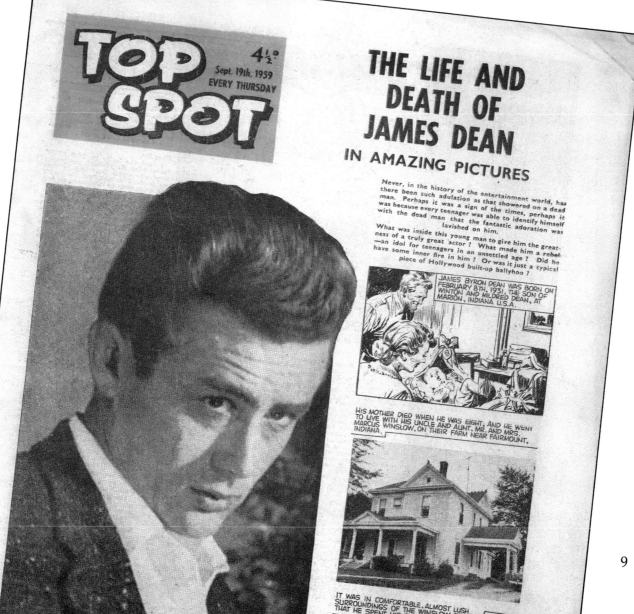

'I tried to get it across to him, to prepare him in some way, but he just didn't seem to take it in. I told him straight one evening, ''Your mother's never coming home again''. All he did was stare at me. Even as a child he wasn't much to talk about his hurts.' – *Winton Dean*

During his visits to the hospital, Jimmy would read aloud to his mother at her bedside.
'I just knew she was asleep before I got through. Then she would wake up and say, ''I am listening, Jimmy. I only had my eyes closed.''' – *Jimmy Dean*

The following year, Mildred Dean died – a loss which was to haunt Jimmy throughout his life. Recalling his emotions at the time of his mother's death:
'It seemed worse than dying itself.' – *Jimmy Dean*

'Having no mother is tough on a kid, you know.' – *Jimmy Dean*

'When I was four or five my mother had me playing the violin – I was a blasted child prodigy. My father came to California and before it was over my mother had me tap-dancing. Not at the same time I was playing the violin. My mother died when I was nine and the violin was buried too.' – *Jimmy Dean*

The sense of sadness and abandonment Jimmy felt at the time of his mother's death never really left him.
'My mother died on me when I was nine years old. What does she expect me to do? Do it all by myself?' – *Jimmy Dean*

'No one helps you, you do it yourself. I don't owe anything to anyone.' – *Jimmy Dean*

'Suffering is good. Suffering is the only way to understand what you're about.' – *Jimmy Dean*

'I used to cry and cry on her grave and say, ''Mother, why did you have to leave me? Why did you leave me? I need you... I want you.''
Okay, well that eventually turned into Jimmy pounding on the grave saying, ''I'll show you for leaving me...fuck you, I'm gonna be so fuckin' great without you!''' – *Jimmy Dean*

Years later, talking about Grace Kelly:
'To me she's the complete mother image, typifying perfection. Maybe she's the kind of person you would like to have had for a mother.' – *Jimmy Dean*

Winton Dean was almost bankrupted by the bills for Mildred's medical treatment, and it was decided that Jimmy should return to Indiana to live with his more prosperous aunt and uncle, Marcus and Ortense Winslow. His mother's coffin, which was to be buried in the family vault, accompanied

Below: Aged 3 Jimmy manages a wistful smile. Below centre: Winton Dean (left) with Ortense and Marcus Winslow, who raised Jimmy after his mother's death. Bottom: Jimmy with the Winslows.

Jimmy on his journey back east, but the little boy never let his grief show.
'He shut it all inside him. The only person he could ever have talked about it with was lying there in the casket.' – *Jimmy's cousin, Joan*

Remembering his mixed feelings when he arrived at his uncle's farm in Fairmount:
'I don't know whether I was looking for a greater source of life and expression...or for blood.' – *Jimmy Dean*

Jimmy settled down to life on the farm and he began to enjoy many of the pursuits of a country boy.
'My uncle's place was a real farm and I worked like crazy as long as someone was watching me. Forty acres of oats made a huge stage and when the audience left I took a nap and nothing got plowed or harrowed. Then I met a friend who lived over in Marion and he taught me how to wrestle and kill cats, and other things boys do behind barns. And I began to live.' – *Jimmy Dean*

Jimmy's lifelong passion for speed was awakened when his uncle bought him a motorcycle.
'If he'd fallen only once, things might have been different. Trouble is, he never got hurt and he never found anything he couldn't do well almost the first time he tried. Just one fall off the bike and maybe he'd have been afraid of speed. But he was without fear' – *Marcus Winslow*

'I used to go out for the cows on the motorcycle. Scared the hell out of them. They'd get to running and their udders would start swinging, and they'd lose a quart of milk.' – *Jimmy Dean*

Jimmy's natural daredevil mentality was encouraged and influenced by the Reverend Dr James de Weerd, a local Wesleyan minister who introduced him to motor racing and bull-fighting.
'I taught Jimmy to believe in personal immortality. He had no fear of death because

he believed, as I do, that death is merely a control of mind over matter.' – *Dr James de Weerd*

De Weerd also became a close confidant of Jimmy's and helped him to come to terms with his mother's death.
'I was up at the cemetery and came across Jimmy weeping at his mother's graveside. Apparently it was the anniversary of her death and he was tidying the grave and was putting flowers on it. He asked me to stay and talk. And then, for the next fifteen minutes said nothing until, suddenly turning to me, he asked, ''Do you think it was my fault she died so young?'' I told him I did not, then he asked if I felt it could have been his father's fault. We were walking slowly towards the gates of the cemetery when Jimmy saw a frail old man trying to improve

The combination of moody outsider and athletic down-home boy was already in evidence by Jimmy's mid-teens, a fact eagerly seized on by magazines and memorials alike.

the appearance of a loved one's grave. Jimmy wiped his eyes and pulled himself together and then went over and offered to help the old guy who was pleased to accept. Jimmy stayed the rest of the afternoon with him and I will always remember that day because it sums up the James Dean that I knew and loved like a son.' – *Dr James de Weerd*

At school, Jimmy showed academic promise, but his grades were always disappointing. His excuse was that he had too many outside interests.
'Why did God put all these things here for us to be interested in?' – *Jimmy Dean*

One of those interests was acting, which had been encouraged by his Aunt Ortense. She took him along to the local Women's Christian Temperance Union where he participated in their drama competitions.
'I felt a need to prove myself and had the facility to do so. Instead of doing little poems I recited gory odes. This made me a straight little harpy in short pants. But I won all the medals the W C T U had to offer. I became pretty proficient.' – *Jimmy Dean*

But the piety of the surroundings disquieted Jimmy:
'The way they had it, you could go to hell

James Dean (centre front) in the school baseball team

14

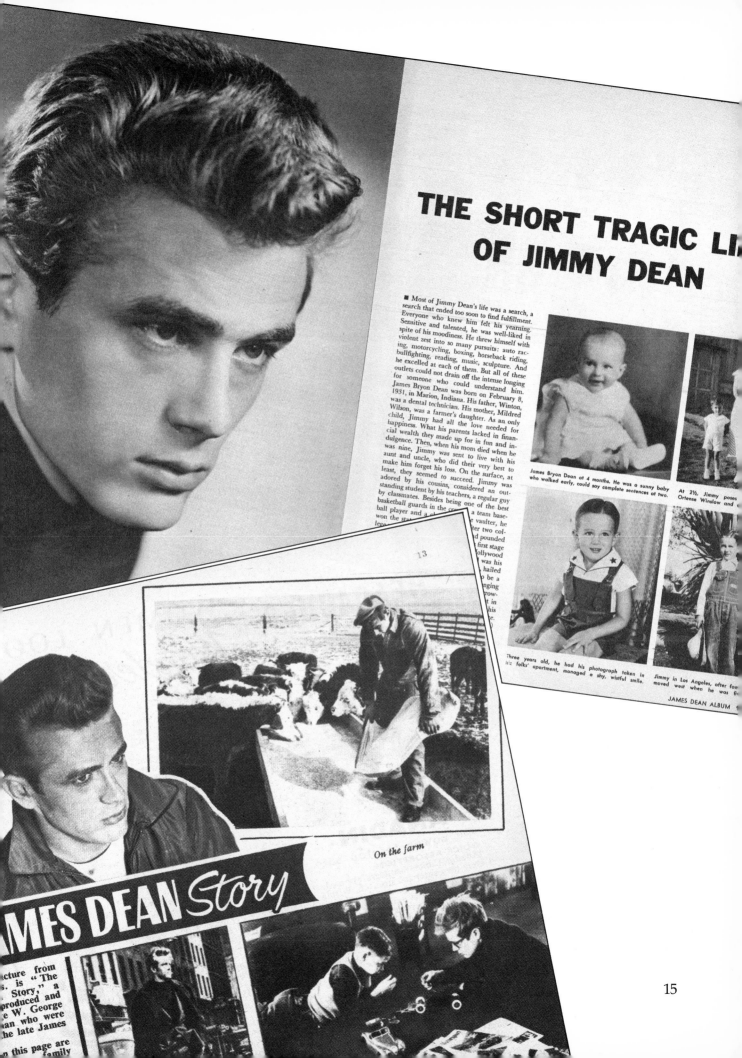

THE SHORT TRAGIC LI[FE] OF JIMMY DEAN

■ Most of Jimmy Dean's life was a search, a search that ended too soon to find fulfillment. Everyone who knew him felt his yearning. Sensitive and talented, he was well-liked in spite of his moodiness. He threw himself with violent zest into so many pursuits: auto racing, motorcycling, boxing, horseback riding, bullfighting, reading, music, sculpture. And he excelled at each of them. But all of these outlets could not drain off the intense longing for someone who could understand him. James Bryon Dean was born on February 8, 1931, in Marion, Indiana. His father, Winton, was a dental technician. His mother, Mildred Wilson, was a farmer's daughter. As an only child, Jimmy had all the love needed for happiness. What his parents lacked in financial wealth they made up for in fun and indulgence. Then, when his mom died when he was nine, Jimmy was sent to live with his aunt and uncle, who did their very best to make him forget his loss. On the surface, at least, they seemed to succeed. Jimmy was adored by his cousins, considered an outstanding student by his teachers, a regular guy by classmates. Besides being one of the best basketball guards in the co[unty], a team baseball player and a cl[ass] vaulter, he won the sta[te] [two col]lege ... Hollywood ... was his ... hailed ... to be a ... nging ... row[th] ... in his ...

James Bryon Dean at 4 months. He was a sunny baby who walked early, could say complete sentences at two.

At 2½, Jimmy poses [with] Ortense Winslow and ...

Three years old, he had his photograph taken in his folks' apartment, managed a shy, wistful smile.

Jimmy in Los Angeles, after fam[ily] moved west when he was fi[rst] ...

JAMES DEAN ALBUM

On the farm

[JA]MES DEAN *Story*

...cture from ... is "The ... Story," a ...roduced and ... W. George ...an who were ...he late James ... this page are ...family

15

just for stepping on a grape.' – *Jimmy Dean*

His natural talent as an actor was spotted at high school by his drama teacher, Adeline Nall, and Jimmy was persuaded to enter the State Forensic League drama contest.
'One of my teachers was a frustrated actress. Through her I entered and won a state oratorical dramatic contest, reciting a Dickens piece called ''The Madman''. About this real gone cat who knocks off several people. It also begins with a scream. I really woke up those judges.' – *Jimmy Dean*

'The decision to act was never prompted. My whole life has been spent in dramatic display of expression.' – *Jimmy Dean*

Jimmy always acknowledged the part chance played in his career. When asked many years later how he happened to turn to acting:

'It was an accident, although I've been involved in some kind of theatrical function or other since I was a child – in school, music, athletics. To me, acting is the most logical way for people's neuroses to manifest themselves, in the great need we have to express ourselves. To my way of thinking, an actor's course is set even before he's out of the cradle.' – *Jimmy Dean*

Jimmy went on to compete in the National Forensic League, held in Longmont, Colorado, where he came sixth. He wouldn't be bound by the rules of the competition and refused to shorten the piece he was reciting. When Adeline Nall warned him that the twelve-minute piece was too long, Jimmy

Far left: James Dean aged 13 with his little cousin Markie. Left: As Frankenstein's monster in a school play. Below: James Dean, front row centre, when President of the School Thespian Society. Bottom: Jimmy revisiting his school stage in 1955.

replied:
'Perfect for *Long*-mont.'

Neither would he dress up for the occasion by putting on a suit and tie.
'This bit I'm doing is a wild one. It's a Dickens thing called ''The Madman'' and I've got to go crazy in it. How the heck can I go crazy in a shirt and tie? It wouldn't work...I don't need to win. Only I can't do the piece if I don't feel like it, and I can't feel like it all duded up.' – *Jimmy Dean*

It became clear that Jimmy was outgrowing the provincial, rural outlook of Fairmount and his adopted family.
'I was never a farmer. I always wanted out of there but I never ran away because I never wanted to hurt anyone.' – *Jimmy Dean*

A poem Jimmy wrote about the town of Fairmount:
'My town likes industrial impotence
My town's small, loves its diffidence
My town thrives on dangerous bigotry
My town's big in the sense of idolotry
My town's innocent, selfistic caper
My town's diligent, reads the newspaper
My town's sweet, I was born bare
My town is not what I am, I am here.'

In his final year at high school, Jimmy refused to apply himself, for fear of what the other kids might say.
'I'd rather not get good grades than be called a sissy.'

He graduated in 1949 at the age of eighteen with good grades, but his 'rebel' reputation was

THE MAN BEHIND THE LEGEND

Many influences formed him, and the remarkable thing about Jimmy was that he was fully as special as his legend

BY KATHRYN TATE

Jimmy was a good-looking youth and started out as an excellent student, but in high school his grades slumped.

Besides school sports, he liked to invent his own games to show off, says former teacher. The girls loved it.

On this rambling farm in Fairmount, Indiana, Jimmy Dean spent most of his early years with his aunt and uncle after the death of his mother. He often took trips back "home." Right, Jimmy was a charming youngster.

FAIRMOUNT HIGH TRACK TEAM

Date	Team		Held	
March 29 — Sweetser			At Sweetser	
April 12 — Mississinewa and Swayzee			At Sweetser	
April 16 — Van Buren			At Fairmount	
April 20 — County			At Marion	
April 23 — Converse Relays			At Converse	
April 30 — Kokomo Relays			At Kokomo	
May 6 — Converse and Montpelier			At Converse	
May 14 — Sectional			At Marion	

The following track boys are ones who were outstanding in events from Fairmount High School.

Earl Scott
Rex Bright
100-220 yard dash .... Charles Lewis, Charles Johnson
Gene Stine, Lawrence Kinch
Jim Grindle

individualism, ... also one of the handsomest and most diabolically attractive men of his .... idolized by women and ....

maintained when his report read:
'Above average, good, but handicapped by a lack of application.'

The family discussed what he would do next. In spite of their misgivings it was obvious that Jimmy had a talent for acting.
'It was becoming plain to all of us that acting was the thing Jimmy was best at. He'd won declamatory contests, even a state one; but the thing that convinced us that he was an actor was his appearance in a church play called *To Them That Sleep In Darkness*. Jimmy played the blind boy. Well, I'll tell you, I wished he wasn't quite so good at it. I cried all the way through.' – *Emma Dean, Jimmy's*

grandmother.

In June 1949, Jimmy left Fairmount to make the journey to his father in Santa Monica, where he planned to further his acting career. Fairmount would never again be home to Jimmy, but he never forgot the importance of those formative school years.
'Whatever abilities I may have crystallised there in high school, when I was trying to prove something to myself – that I could do it, I suppose.' – *Jimmy Dean*

19

Chapter 2

THE EARLY STRUGGLES

'There's only one true form of greatness
for a man. If a man can bridge the gap
between life and death, I mean if he can
live on after he's died, then, maybe, he
was a great man.' Jimmy Dean

When Jimmy arrived in Los Angeles, he immediately joined a local summer stock company and performed in its production of the musical melodrama The Romance of Scarlet Gulch. *But he did not fit in with his fellow actors.*

'The most catty, criticising, narcissistic bunch of people you ever saw, always at each other's throats. But let an outsider try to interfere and they flock together like a bunch of long-lost buddies...What a life. I learnt a lot from them, I've just got to be patient, I guess. They never made it until their twenties, thirties and even forties.' – *Jimmy Dean*

His father set about trying to discourage him from his plan of studying theatre arts at the University of California, Los Angeles (UCLA). Jimmy at last relented and opted for a 'sensible' degree course in law at the local Santa Monica City College. Immediately he threw himself into the dramatic

productions of the college.

'He was always polite and thoughtful; his enthusiasm for everything that pertained to the theatre was boundless...One day in class Jimmy read some scenes from Edgar Allen Poe's *Tell-tale Heart*. He was magnificent – but then he always had a spectacular emotion for any scene he played. Later, during that same class I asked Jimmy to read some scenes from *Hamlet*. That night when I returned home I informed my husband that I had finally found the right student to play Hamlet as I felt it should be played.' – *Jean Owen, a drama teacher at Santa Monica*

After Jimmy had read the Hamlet *scenes to her, Jean Owen asked him whether he had studied Shakespeare at Stratford-upon-Avon along with the great Shakespearian actors, Laurence Olivier and John Gielgud. But his training for the part,*

JIMMY'S AWARDS

Here is the record of Jimmy's achievements in the short span of his acting career—and the recognition he won . . .

He became the youngest person admitted to Actors' Studio.

He appeared in two radio productions: "Stars Over Hollywood" and "Alias Jane Doe".

He appeared in ten television productions: "Hill Number One"; Studio One; Philco Television Playhouse; Schlitz Television Playhouse; Martin Kane; Tales of Tomorrow; The Kate Smith Show; Campbell Sound Stage; T-Men In Action; Hallmark Playhouse.

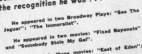

He appeared in two Broadway Plays: "See The Jaguar"; "The Immoralist".

He appeared in two movies: "Fixed Bayonets" and "Somebody Stole My Gal".

He starred in three movies: "East of Eden"; "Rebel Without A Cause"; "Giant".

In four years he did all this, and died. For this the press, the public, and the professionals in his profession have awarded him the following honors to date:

The Daniel Blum Award . . . most promising stage personality............1953-1954

The Antoinette Perry Award ("Tony," best supporting actor on Broadway)........1953-1954

The Filmdom's Famous Fives Award.........1955

The Motion Picture Academy of Arts and Sciences Nomination (best actor in "East of Eden") 1956

The Motion Picture Academy of Arts and Sciences Nomination (best actor in "Giant")............1957

Photoplay Award for outstanding performance in "East of Eden" and "Rebel Without A Cause"............1956

Modern Screen Special Achievement Award 1956

The Filmdom's Famous Fives Award.........1956

The Audience Award Nomination most promising new male personality............1956

The Audience Award Nomination for best actor 1956

The Audience Award (best actor) over 15,000,000 plurality............1956

The French Film Academy's award as best foreign actor ("East of Eden")............1956

The French Film Academy's highest award, The Crystal Star............1956

The English Academy award—best actor 1956

The French "Winged Victory" award for best actor, "Giant"............1957

The "Pierre"—260,000 Fan Club as best actor, 1957

Voted "World's Favorite Actor for 1956" by the Hollywood Foreign Press Association....1957

Voted "Top Foreign Actor" for his starring role in "Rebel Without a Cause" by the Tokyo Movie Fans Association............1957

Voted the 1956 Million Pearl Award as the top foreign actor by Japan............1957

Awarded the best male star trophy for 1956, by the Yokohama Movie Circle Council............1957

Awarded the Certificate of Merit as the best foreign actor of 1956 by the Yokohama Movie Circle Council............1957

Awarded a Diploma as the best male performer by Cine-Revere, Brussels, Belgium............1957

Awarded a Statuette by Elokvva Journalist, Finnish Film-Journalists............1957

THE END

19

In this hitherto unpublished picture, we catch a glimpse of the deep currents of feeling and compassion that animated JIMMY's genius.

as he told her, was far more lowly.
'I practised for years in the middle of a wheat field in Indiana.' – *Jimmy Dean*

Through the years, Jimmy had always felt that he had a special affinity for the role of Hamlet.
'I want to do Hamlet soon. Only a young man can play Hamlet as he was – with the naiveté. Laurence Olivier plays it safe. Something is lost when the older men play him. They anticipate the answers. You don't feel Hamlet is thinking – just declaiming. Sonority of voice and technique the older men have, but this kind of Hamlet isn't the stumbling, feeling, reaching, searching boy he really was.' – *Jimmy Dean*

A fellow student at the Santa Monica College recognised the same 'stumbling, feeling, reaching, searching boy' in Jimmy's own personality:
'He was shy and awkward, peering through big horn-rimmed glasses at a world that baffled him.'

In 1950, Jimmy became a law student at UCLA with theatre arts as his subsidiary subject.
'Just for the hell of it, I signed up for a pre-law course at UCLA. That did call for a certain knowledge of histrionics. I even joined a fraternity on campus.' – *Jimmy Dean*

24

But his passion for acting soon dominated his student activities. Jimmy had determined to become an actor in the summer of 1950 when he saw Marlon Brando on screen in The Men. *The mean and moody image of Brando hypnotised him, and was to provide a powerful influence in the formative years of his career.*

'Dean was never a friend of mine. But he had an *idée fixe* about me. Whatever I did, he did. He was always trying to get close to me. He used to call up on the phone. I'd listen to him talking to the answering service, asking for me, leaving messages, but I never spoke up. I never called him back.' – *Marlon Brando*

'Dean's hero was Marlon Brando and he tried to outdo Brando in the non-conformist game. The difference between their behaviour was that Brando often put on an outrageous act for a laugh. But Dean was self-destructive, masochistic – sick.' – *Elia Kazan, director of* East of Eden

Jimmy was overjoyed when he landed a part in the UCLA production of Macbeth.
'The biggest thrill of my life came three weeks ago, after a week of gruelling auditions for UCLA's four major theatrical productions, the major one being Shakespeare's *Macbeth* which will be presented in Royce Hall (seats 1600). After the auditioning of 367 actors and actresses I came up with a wonderful lead in *Macbeth*, the character being Malcolm (huge part)...' – *Jimmy Dean, in a letter to his aunt and uncle*

'I directed Dean in *Macbeth*. He wasn't at UCLA very long; he just worked on that one show. I didn't think he was happy at school. I guess the university life was too slow for him. I got the feeling he wanted to act and nothing more than that, so he didn't take to the rest of the academic requirements.' – *Dr Walden Boyle, a professor at UCLA*

Jimmy's assessment of the value of UCLA for aspiring actors:
'Too many directors and not enough actors.'

There was little praise for Jimmy's acting talents from the university newspaper:
'Malcolm failed to show any growth, and would have made a hollow king.'

Actors' agent Isabel Draesmar was talent-spotting in the audience and recognised a greater promise in Jimmy's performance. She came backstage after the show and offered to represent him, an offer which was hastily accepted.
His burgeoning acting activities did not go down well with his beer-drinking, athletic fraternity, and he was duly thrown out after he had a fight with two members who were taunting him about his dramatic leanings.
'I busted a couple of guys in the nose and got myself kicked out.' – *Jimmy Dean*

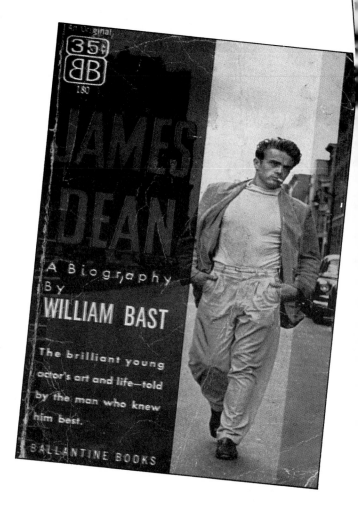

This meant Jimmy had nowhere to live, so he suggested to fellow UCLA student Bill Bast that they look for an apartment together. The pair found a place in Santa Monica, and, under the patronage of Isabel Draesmar, they started on the interminable round of auditions and bit parts. Jimmy decided to drop his academic studies completely.
'I wanted to be a professional actor. I couldn't take that tea-sipping academic bull.' – *Jimmy Dean*

By this stage, he was totally committed to becoming a great actor and would not contemplate the possibility of achieving mediocrity. It was the beginning of an uncompromising path towards immortality.
'I figure there's nothing you can't do if you

put everything into it. The only thing that stops people from getting what they want is themselves. They put too many barriers in their paths. It's like they're afraid to succeed. In a way, I guess I know why. There's a terrific amount of responsibility that goes with success, and the greater the success, the greater the responsibility. People don't want that kind of responsibility.

'But I think, if you're not afraid, if you take everything you are, everything worthwhile in you, and direct it at one goal, one ultimate mark, you've got to get there. If you start accepting the world, letting things happen to you, around you, things will happen like you never dreamed they'd happen.

'That's why I'm going to stick to this thing. I don't just want to be a good actor. I don't

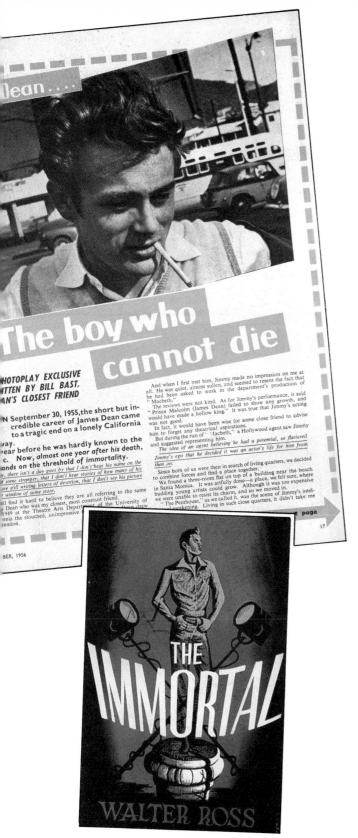

The boy who cannot die

PHOTOPLAY EXCLUSIVE
WRITTEN BY BILL BAST,
DEAN'S CLOSEST FRIEND

ON September 30, 1955, the short but incredible career of James Dean came to a tragic end on a lonely California highway.

A year before he was hardly known to the public. Now, almost one year after his death, he stands on the threshold of immortality.

There isn't a day goes by that I don't hear his name on the lips of some stranger, that I don't hear stories of how many of his fans are still writing letters of devotion, that I don't see his picture in the window of some store.

You'll find it hard to believe they are all referring to the same Jimmy Dean who was my closest, most constant friend.

In 1949 at the Theatre Arts Department of the University of California the slouched, unimpressive Dean drew no attention.

And when I first met him, Jimmy made no impression on me at all. He was quiet, almost sullen, and seemed to resent the fact that he had been asked to work in the department's production of " Macbeth."

The reviews were not kind. As for Jimmy's performance, it said " Prince Malcolm (James Dean) failed to show any growth, and would have made a hollow king." It was true that Jimmy's acting was not good.

In fact, it would have been wise for some close friend to advise him to forget any theatrical aspirations.

But during the run of " Macbeth," a Hollywood agent saw Jimmy and suggested representing him.

The idea of an agent believing he had a potential, so flattered Jimmy's ego that he decided it was an actor's life for him from then on.

Since both of us were then in search of living quarters, we decided to combine forces and find a place together.

We found a three-room flat on top of a building near the beach in Santa Monica. It was artfully done—a place, we felt sure, where budding young artists could grow. Although it was too expensive we were unable to resist its charm, and so we moved in.

" The Penthouse," as we called it, was the scene of Jimmy's intellectual awakening. Living in such close quarters, it didn't take me

next page →

17

OCTOBER, 1956

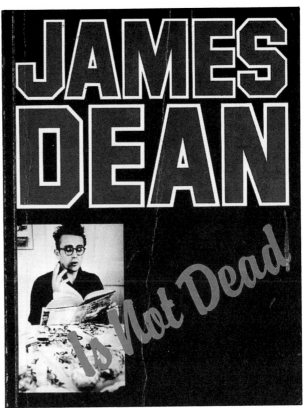

even want to be just the best. I want to grow and grow, grow so tall that nobody can reach me. Not to prove anything, but just to go where you ought to go when you devote your whole life and all you are to one thing.

'Maybe that sounds crazy or egocentric or something, but I think there's only one true form of greatness for a man. If a man can bridge the gap between life and death, I mean if he can live on after he's died, then maybe he was a great man. When they talk about success, they talk about reaching the top. Well, there is no top. You've got to go on and on, never stop at any point. To me, the only success, the only greatness for a man is immortality. To have your work remembered in history, to leave something in this world that will last for centuries - that's greatness.

'I want to grow away from all the petty little world we exist in. I want to leave it all behind, all the petty little thoughts about the unimportant little things, things that'll be forgotten in a hundred years from now, anyway. There's a level somewhere where everything is solid and important. I'm going to try to reach up there and find a place I know is pretty close to perfect, a place where this whole messy world should be, could be, if it'd just take time to learn.' – *Jimmy Dean*

He took his first tentative step when he got the part of St John the Baptist in a TV series

27

scheduled for Easter called Hill Number One.
*but his performance was not stunning and he
himself recalls playing the part:*
'Like an old Jewish actor.'

*Inexperience and nerves had much to do with his
unimpressive screen début. He found difficulty in
applying the techniques he had learnt in James
Whitmore's informal acting classes to an actual
performance. Whitmore was a well respected actor
of his day, famous for his Method acting.*
'I build up this head of steam like in
Jimmy Whitmore's exercises, but where in
class you then let it rip, on film you've got to
keep it bottled up. It makes me look like my

bladder's bursting.' – *Jimmy Dean*

*Whitmore, though, was a positive and lasting
influence on Jimmy's development as an actor.*
'I owe a lot to him. I guess you can
say he saved me when I got all mixed up. He
told me I didn't know the difference between
acting as a soft job, and acting as a difficult
art. I needed to learn these differences.
People ask me these ridiculous questions
like, "When did you decide to become an
actor?"...I don't know that there was ever
any such time. I realised I was an actor
because of James Whitmore. There's always
someone who opens up your eyes. For me,

Left: An early contact sheet for casting directors.

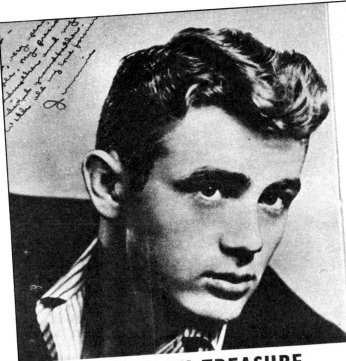

A FAMILY TREASURE

... is this portrait of James Dean at the age of 20. He inscribed it across one corner: "To two very special people. My precious grandmother and my wonderful grandfather. With all my love forever. Jimmie."

do, but nothing really definite fixed in his mind—except that he knew he would like it to have something to do with acting.

"But suppose you do like acting, son," argued his dad, "will you be happy leading an actor's life? Why don't you study law? That way your acting ability will be of real use to you."

Jimmy realised his pop's advice was pretty good. For it is quite true that to be a bit of an actor would come in useful to a young lawyer who often has to argue cases in a crowded courtroom.

So he enrolled himself as a student at California University, planning to study law *and* dramatic art. To support himself while he was studying, he took on the job of running a cinema projector for special education classes.

But the study of law was not for Jimmy. It wasn't exciting enough by far. It had none of that tingling 'get-up-and-go' which he always demanded from life. Dry legal studies made him yawn in boredom. Slouching about the university grounds in shabby clothes, his eyes always fixed on the ground, he appeared a lonely, lost kind of figure.

His room mate at the time, Bill Bast, says: "He wasn't very happy at the university." But it mustn't be thought that Jimmy cut himself off from people there —his pleasant manners and homely country drawl won him many friends. It was just that he realised he had no interest in law.

Like Jimmy, Bill Bast was also deeply interested in acting and the theatre, and he persuaded

Hollywood actor James Whitmore to organise a voluntary class at the university. The class was to be patterned after the world-famous Lee Strasberg's Actors' Studio in New York.

Jimmy joined—and was like a man dying of thirst given a long refreshing drink. This—acting, acting, acting—was the life for him. This was what he had really been born for. He threw himself into Whitmore's theatre classes with an intensity that was almost frightening to his fellow students, because he took them so seriously, worked so hard.

He was proud of his new-found vocation as an actor, and resented any slurs upon acting as a profession.

Once, at a college party, when some students made sneering cracks about long-haired actors not even having strength enough to lift a glass above their elbows, Jimmy slugged a couple of them on the nose and got himself thrown out.

By now, with his head full of theatre, he had forgotten what little he had ever learnt about law, and had no more idea of becoming a lawyer than of taking a trip to the moon. He was never actually expelled from the university, though. He just floated away absent-mindedly and forgot to go back.

The fair-haired kid with the strange, intense look and a temper that was apt to flare up suddenly, knew now, with overpowering certainty, just what he was going to do with his life.

Act.

9

Moody New Star

HOOSIER JAMES DEAN EXCITES HOLLYWOOD

Most exciting actor to hit Hollywood since Marlon Brando is the moody, 24-year-old recluse above, James Dean of Fairmount, Ind. His performance in Elia Kazan's forthcoming *East of Eden*, reminiscent of Brando but distinctively his own, has already won him a starring role in another big picture, *Giant*. His militantly independent offstage behavior and his scorn for movie convention have studio executives at Warner Bros. apprehensive. In *Eden* his skillful portrayal of the elder son of a California rancher stems partly from his own complex personality and from elements in his own farm-bred early life.

Though shy of publicity which he feels might show him in a false light, Dean recently permitted a friend, Dennis Stock, to go back home with him to make photographs. How he reacted to life on the farm and how it contrasts with his new one is reported on these pages.

IN SUNDAY BEST Dean reads, as he used to when a child after Sunday school, in uncle's barn.

IN "EAST OF EDEN" Dean, here in scene with Julie Harris, plays role of unloved problem child.

that's Whitmore. He made me see myself. He opened me up, gave me the key.' – *Jimmy Dean*

After his brief moment of glory as St John, the work dried up and Jimmy sank into a fit of melancholy.

'Jimmy became subject to more frequent periods of depression and would slip off into a silent mood at least once each day...If I had thought it difficult to communicate with him at other times in the past, I had never known such lack of communication as existed during his fits of depression...He would sit in his room, sit there and stare into space for hours. I made several attempts to get through to him, but rarely got more than a grunt or a distant stare for a response.' – *Bill Bast*

The relationship between Jimmy and Bast, which was already tense, broke up completely when

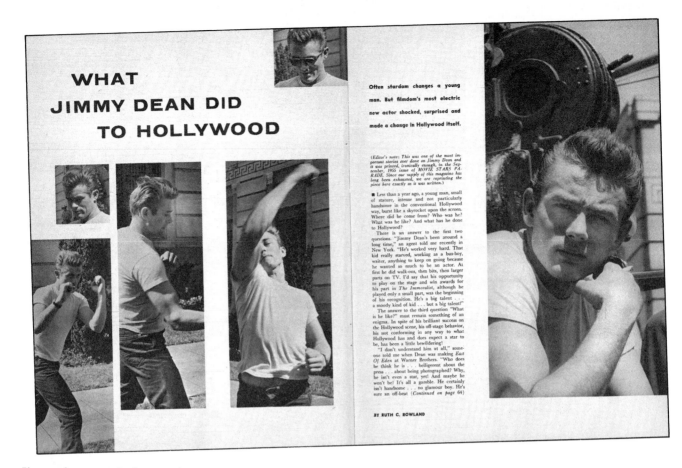

WHAT JIMMY DEAN DID TO HOLLYWOOD

Often stardom changes a young man. But filmdom's most electric new actor shocked, surprised and made a change in Hollywood itself.

(Editor's note: This was one of the most important stories ever done on Jimmy Dean and it was printed, ironically enough, in the September, 1955 issue of MOVIE STARS PARADE. Since our supply of this magazine has long been exhausted, we are reprinting the piece here exactly as it was written.)

■ Less than a year ago, a young man, small of stature, intense and not particularly handsome in the conventional Hollywood way, burst like a skyrocket upon the screen. Where did he come from? Who was he? What was he like? And what has he done to Hollywood?

There is an answer to the first two questions. "Jimmy Dean's been around a long time," an agent told me recently in New York. "He's worked very hard. That kid really starved, working as a bus-boy, waiter, anything to keep on going because he wanted so much to be an actor. At first he did walk-ons, then bits, then larger parts on TV. I'd say that his opportunity to play on the stage and win awards for his part in *The Immoralist*, although he played only a small part, was the beginning of his recognition. He's a big talent . . . a moody kind of kid . . . but a big talent!"

The answer to the third question "What is he like?" must remain something of an enigma. In spite of his brilliant success on the Hollywood scene, his off-stage behavior, his not conforming in any way to what Hollywood has and does expect a star to be, has been a little bewildering!

"I don't understand him at all," someone told me when Dean was making *East Of Eden* at Warner Brothers. "Who does he think he is . . . belligerent about the press . . . about being photographed? Why, he isn't even a star, yet! And maybe he won't be! It's all a gamble. He certainly isn't handsome . . . no glamour boy. He's sure an off-beat *(Continued on page 64)*

BY RUTH C. ROWLAND

Jimmy began to fool around with Bast's girlfriend, Beverly Wills, the daughter of comedienne Joan Davis. Jimmy was forced to move out of the apartment and finally found a place to stay with a young CBS director, Rogers Brackett. Brackett found his friend work which eventually led to Jimmy's first part in a film, Fixed Bayonets. It was not the glamorous 'break' he had hoped for. 'There we were, all crouched down behind this hill, covered with dirt and sweat. And it was night, raining, real Hollywood, you know. I had exactly one line. It went, "It's a rear guard coming back." What a part!' – Jimmy Dean

He then secured another bit part in Sailor Beware, a comedy starring Dean Martin and Jerry Lewis which gave Jimmy a brief but valuable taste of professional acting.
'I remember the first time I had to get the make-up on. I sat there and the make-up guy said, "Put your head back and keep your chin up", and he slapped it on and I knew then, squinting at the mirror, where and what I was

supposed to be.' – Jimmy Dean

But in front of the camera Jimmy had to channel most of his energies into overcoming stage fright. 'Maybe I smoked too much or maybe I was drinking too much coffee, but I felt sick sure enough, and I thought I'd puke all over Jerry Lewis.' – Jimmy Dean

But Jimmy was still far away from stardom, with even bit-parts becoming rare and sporadic. He had also become deeply disillusioned with the smart Hollywood cocktail set that Rogers Brackett had introduced him to in the hope that he would make useful contacts.
'You know, it gets sickening. The other day we were sitting by the pool and I made a bet with Rogers that the name of LaRue or Mocambo would be dropped at least fifteen times within the next hour. We kept count and I won. What a pile of shit.' – Jimmy Dean

'What a pile of hogwash. With all their power and wealth they've got it in their heads that

30

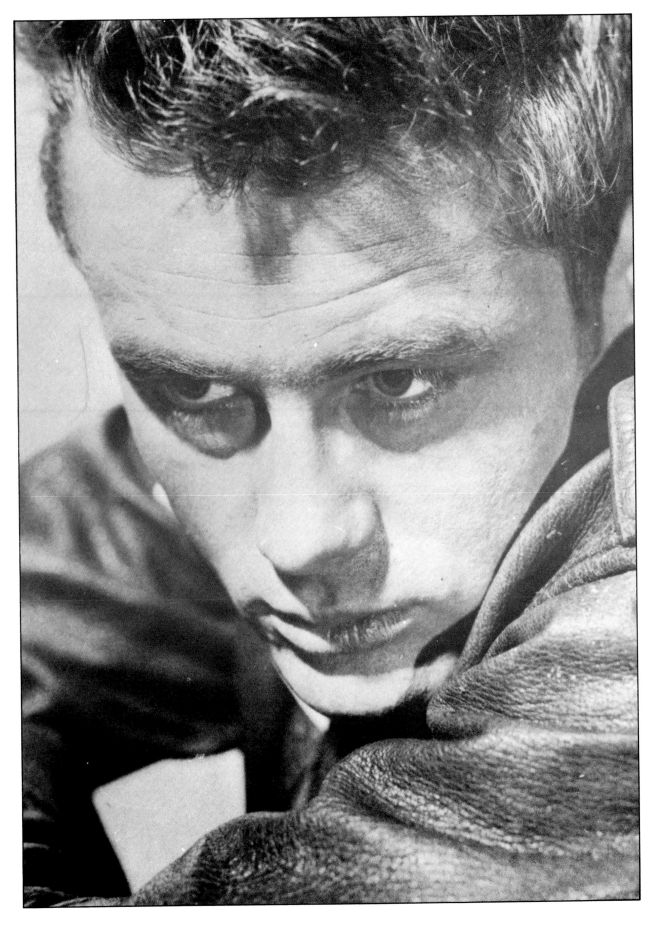

they're gods. This town's full of them. They get these poor kids, saps like me, and make them perform. You know – run around like court jesters charming the pants off important people...I thought it might pay off. But it doesn't take long to find out it won't. I'm not performing for any of them. Not any more. And if I can't make it on my talent, I don't want to make it at all.' – *Jimmy Dean*

He was running out of money and hope.
'If only I could accomplish something before I die.' – *Jimmy Dean to his girlfriend, Beverly Wills*

'He'd walk into our living room, and promptly slump down in my mother's favourite armchair, his foot dangling over the side, and sit like that for hours without saying a word. The only action we'd see out of him was when he'd reach for the fruit bowl. He was always hungry.' – *Beverly Wills*

To make matters worse, Jimmy was surrounded by that sweet smell of success which pervaded Hollywood.
'It was going on around me all the time and, man, I'd stop somewhere like in the windows of that Coffee Dan's on Vine Street because that was across the road from NBC and I was always trying to get something over there, if it was only a little part and I didn't care what it was, but there were times I looked at myself in the window and I looked weird, man, weird...It was like I wasn't real any more, and here I was – this kind of kid going around, but Hollywood was coming up over me. Once when that shit-car wasn't running, I had blood in my socks because I got blisters from walking around all over there – no matter how much I'd go around and see these people it wasn't going to happen for me and I got lost. Simple as that – I got lost.' – *Jimmy Dean*

Below: Jimmy relaxing in New York with his ubiquitous bongo drums. Left: Grabbing a bite at a Times Square snack stand.

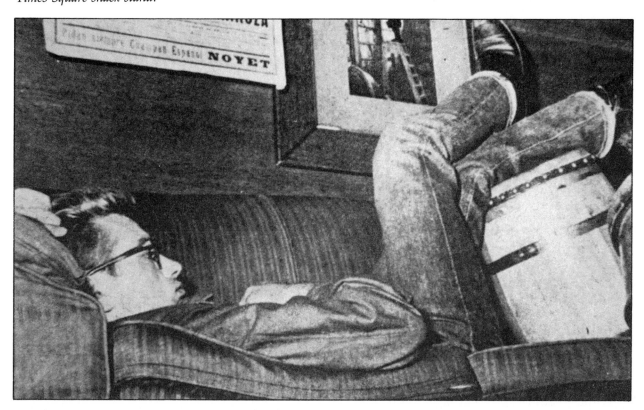

'He was so beaten-down looking. Jimmy was like a teenage hobo, like all the misfits he started playing on television a little later. But really he wasn't that way. Sure, he used to stand around in Santa Monica with a hangdog look or he'd be walking around the area eating a hotdog and you'd think he was just looking for action. We used to walk up and down the beach strip too, where the crummiest gay bars were. We'd drink a few times, and he told me he had a great disappointment in Hollywood. He said, ''Not because it hasn't discovered me. I'm not that stupid, but I'm sick of trying to do something, trying to make something happen,'' and it was beginning to seem like it wasn't going to happen for him.' – *An actor friend*

'There's only one really bad thing in the world and that's standing still – stagnating.' – *Jimmy Dean*

Jimmy's mentor, James Whitmore, suggested that he try New York as a fresh source of inspiration and opportunity. Jimmy didn't need much persuading as he had been fascinated by the allure of New York since 1949.
'Three ball parks. Three ball parks in one town. Geez – I'm coming to Manhattan some time.' – *Jimmy Dean*

To Bill Bast about his reasons for leaving Hollywood and going to New York.
'I can't stomach this dung hole any more.' – *Jimmy Dean*

'They'll never really give me a chance out here, I'm not the bobby-sox type, and I'm not the romantic leading man type either. Can you imagine me making love to Lana Turner? – *Jimmy Dean*

But Jimmy was still determined to become a great actor. He felt that fate had decreed it.
'I got to be faithful to her [fate]. In any case it's predestined that I'm going to make it and that I'm going to make it like Marlon did – that I'm going to be a gigantic movie star.' – *Jimmy Dean*

Chapter 3

NEW YORK

'This town's the end. They've got
everything in the world here. I mean, if
you let things happen there's no telling
where you can go.' Jimmy Dean

'Jimmy was beautiful. There are some beautiful people you can't resist. He was one of them. And in New York he was hungry and eager and he'd do almost anything to get a little bit ahead.' – *A West Coast TV director*

Having stopped off to visit Marcus and Ortense Winslow in Fairmount, Jimmy arrived in Manhattan in autumn 1951 with only $200 which had been lent to him by the Rev de Weerd. He checked into a YMCA hostel and began to feel engulfed by the impersonality of the Big City.
'New York overwhelmed me. For the first few weeks I only strayed a couple of blocks from my hotel off Times Square. I would see three movies a day in an attempt to escape my loneliness and depression. I spent $150 of my limited funds just on seeing movies.' – *Jimmy Dean*

Jimmy later wrote to a lover, Barbara Glenn, about the seedy New York environment he lived in.
'In the pensiveness of night the cheap, monotonous shrill, symbolic, sensual beat of suggestive drums tatoos orgyistic images on my brain. The smell of gin and 90% beer, entwine with the sometimes suspenseful, slow, sometimes labored static, sometimes motionless, sometimes painfully rigid, till finally the long-awaited for jerks and convulsions that fill the now thick chewing gum haze with a mist of sweat, fling the patrons into a fit of supressed joy. The fated 7 days a week bestial virgin bows with the poise of a drunken pavlova. Rivulets of stale perspiration glide from and between her once well-formed anatomy to the anxious, welcoming front-row celebrities who lap it up with infamous glee. The Aura of Horror. I live above it and below it...It is my Divine Comedy. The Dante of 52nd Street. There is no peace in our world. I love you.
'I would like to write about nicer things or fiction but we shouldn't avoid reality should we? The things I have just written are the truth. They are very hard to write about. I

am lonely. Forgive me. I am lonely.' – *Jimmy Dean*

He started on the treadmill of trying to get established as an actor with the New York film and television companies.
'You won't believe how I used to walk around and try to see these people, I mean the ones that had position and the ones that were doing the casting, and I knew there were parts being cast that I was perfect for.' – *Jimmy Dean*

Jimmy soon forged a close relationship with a dancer called Dizzy Sheridan.
'When we met I was ready to be involved. I guess he was too. He seemed very 'lost' which is attractive. I was working with two boys at the same time – we were trying to get a dance trio together – and he came to see me and that clinched it for him, because I was a good dancer. But we reached for each other; we really did.' – *Dizzy Sheridan*

James Dean's pal, Nick Adams, recalls his favorite stories of...

Jimmy's happiest moments

All the tension went out of Jimmy when he was with kids, and he'd play with them by the hour. Maybe because at heart he was such a kid himself.

He loved animals because he said, "They accept you on your own terms." They tickled him because they would do just what they wanted to and didn't give a darn. Like Jim.

He got a kick out of trying anything new. If it was dangerous like bull-fighting, all the better. If he looked silly, like at ballet dancing—he was the first to laugh at himself.

Photos by Dennis Stock: Magnum

■ I wish someone would explain human beings some day. Why is it that whenever I think of Jimmy Dean, who loved the fun of life much more than he loved life itself, I feel like crying? I mean, the first guy to hoot at me, if he saw me, would be Jimmy himself. I remember his reaction one afternoon when we worked in *Rebel Without A Cause*, and we all argued against his decision to use a real knife, instead of a prop, in the famous knife fight scene. All we had to do was catch the look in his eyes as he stared in protest at us, to know that a prop would be too dull, alone unrealistic, as far as he was concerned.

So he might get cut. So what? So he did get cut—and he was delighted with the feeling of satisfaction that came to him, a feeling based not only on the fact that he had lived his role more than he had pretended it, but that there was a kick to this way of acting, as there should be to everything a fellow pitches in to do—and no matter the cost.

I think my sadness comes because nobody seems to have remembered this Jimmy Dean—or talks about this Jimmy Dean, the fun-loving Dean. The Jimmy Dean I knew was intelligent enough to know that the truth in life comes out in its laughter, and so he lived mostly in laughter when he was with his friends (and, as I later found out, when he was with favorite members of his family). It was true *(Continued on page 30)*

'When I first met Jimmy, he looked like a straggly, hungry kid who needed a friend. After, I found he always looked that way.' – *Dizzy Sheridan*

'He had a pair of jeans and a raincoat...a brown suit that he never wore. But he had a magnificent face. And I always told him I liked him better without his glasses. They were always slipping down. He was shorter than I was, you know. But he was intense, and that was also attractive. And at the same time very tender. Now that's not the Jimmy Dean you've probably heard about.' – *Dizzy Sheridan*

The lovers shared an apartment on 72nd Street for a while until poverty forced Jimmy to move out and live with a friend of Rogers Brackett, Jim Sheldon, a television director. Jimmy won the admiration of actors' agent Jane Deacy, another contact of Brackett's, and persuaded her to take him on – a partnership which was to last throughout his career. His first role was as an off-stage stooge stuntman in the TV series Beat the Clock. *Soon he was landing bit-parts in many of the second-rate TV drama series which were springing up in those early days of television, but still work was sporadic and money was scarce. Television writer Frank Wayne remembers that Jimmy was forced to ask if he could eat the tapioca pudding being used in a commercial after shooting had finished.*

Jimmy Dean: 'Hey, Frank, if you're going to throw that pudding away, can I have it?'
Frank Wayne: 'You sure you want to eat a load of tapioca?'
Jimmy Dean: 'Man, anything would taste good right now. I haven't had anything to eat in two days.'

In the summer of 1952, Bill Bast arrived in New York and the two of them decided to share a room together at the Iroquois Hotel on West 44th Street, next door to the more famous Algonquin Hotel. Jimmy was quick to explain to his old friend the

buzz he got out of this fast-paced city.
'I've discovered a whole new world here, a whole new way of thinking...this town's the end. They've got everything in the world here. I mean, if you let things happen, there's no telling where you can go. It's talent that counts here. You've got to stay with it or get lost. I like it.' – *Jimmy Dean*

Comparing New York with Hollywood:
'Don't get me wrong. I'm not one of the wise ones who try to put Hollywood down. It just happens that I fit into the cadence and pace better here as far as living goes. New York is vital, above all fertile. They're a little harder to find, maybe, but out there in Hollywood, behind all that brick and mortar, there are human beings, just as sensitive to fertility. The problem for this cat – myself – is not to get lost'– *Jimmy Dean*

A turning point in Jimmy's fortunes came that summer when he bumped into an attractive young blonde called Christine White in the office of Jane Deacy, his agent. Christine was preparing her script for an audition at the Actors Studio - a drama school run by Lee Strasberg and Elia Kazan which was hailed as the Mecca of Method Acting. Jimmy had long cherished a dream of being admitted into the Studio's famed portals and following in the footsteps of some of its most celebrated students, among them Marilyn Monroe, Montgomery Clift and Marlon Brando. So it was not long before he had persuaded Christine to write in a second part for her script and the pair began to spend a lot of time together preparing.
'Did I ever have an affair with him? I always say "Yes", and I always say "No", ...because I don't think I'll ever answer that. But we were very close. We were soul mates...'
– *Christine White*

Left: Jimmy in Times Square. Dennis Stock's famous photo-essay for Life *Magazine helped create the Dean myth. Below: Jimmy (third from right) at an Actors Studio session.*

Competition was always intense for a place at the Studio, but out of 150 applicants Jimmy and Chris were the only two to actually gain places.
'Dean made an excellent impression at audition. He never again performed for us as well as for that audition.' – *Lee Strasberg*

In exalted mood Jimmy wrote to Marcus and Ortense to tell them the news.
'I have made great strides in my craft. After months of auditioning I am very proud to announce that I am a member of the Actors Studio. The greatest school of theatre. It houses great people like Marlon Brando, Julie Harris, Arthur Kennedy, Elia Kazan, Mildred Dunnock, Kevin McCarthy, Monty Clift, June Havoc and on and on and on. Very few get into it, and it's absolutely free. It's the best thing that can happen to an actor. I am one of the youngest to belong... If I can keep this

up and nothing interferes with my progress, one of these days I might be able to contribute something to the world...' – *Jimmy Dean*

The maestro of the Actors Studio – Lee Strasberg – aimed to teach his students a new approach to acting, which involved a far deeper understanding of the character they were playing. He encouraged them not to 'play' or 'imitate' the character at all, but rather to 'become' the part by achieving a total sympathy with the character. Strasberg's methods for developing this included 'assassinations' of an actor's performance in front of the other members of the class, so that everyone could learn from one person's mistakes. Jimmy found this level of intense and very personal criticism extremely hard to take, and is reputed to have walked out after a particularly heavy session.
'I don't know what's inside me. I don't know what happens when I act – inside. But if I

"He wasn't impressed with the work he had done in his TV jobs...."

JIMMY DEAN RETURNS

CONTINUED

But on the other hand, I couldn't, I just couldn't go on much longer like this, in this prison my life in New York had become!

I felt trapped and helpless—and hopeless.

Then, one afternoon, all this changed.

Everything changed with a sale I made in the hardware department at Macy's.

It was the most important sale I made all the time I was there. I think it was the most important sale anyone ever made at Macy's.

I was standing at my usual station this afternoon, looking at nothing, thinking nothing, feeling tired and dull, when someone said "Hi."

I looked up. A young man was standing opposite me, smiling at me.

"I want to buy a can-opener," he said. "Not that old-fashioned kind of can-opener where you've got to stab it in like a dagger and use all your strength

14

THIS WAS HIS GREATNESS

Enormous talent and
the ambition to be
a truly good actor
made James Dean
a star.
His career climb
started in New York.
Then Hollywood gave him
the roles and acclaim
that made him famous

To supplement his meager income while he was studying at the Actors Studio, Dean did television work. Here, he plays a romantic scene with co-star Pat Hardy.

Jimmy Dean was filled with ambition. He wanted more than anything else in the world to become an actor, a great actor. But Holly-

His first Broadway role was in *See The Jaguar*, which was considered an artistic success by the New York drama critics, but which failed financially. On the basis of his perform-

The pictures on these pages are from the U.S. Steel Hour Show. "The Thief."

Far left: Jimmy had tuition on the bongos from Cyril Jackson in a music studio off Times Square. Left: Memorial Magazine articles look back over his early career in New York.

In the random television bit parts that came his way Jimmy would try to apply the techniques of method acting he had learnt at the Actors Studio.
'I was working for the director who was casting for show and Jimmy came in for an audition. As the actors were waiting to get called to read, he flopped down on the floor and rested his chin on his hands and started reading the script. Most of the actors and actresses just sat around chewing the fat with each other. One of them said to me, "Get him out of here." I asked why. Maybe it was unseemly conduct to them or something? I guess it could be a bore having to step over him. But he wasn't in anyone's way, so I just didn't say anything.
'Jimmy just lay there and laughed. When it came time to read for the part, he did that – sprawled out on the floor for the scene. So, you see, he wasn't just lying around waiting for an audition, he was making a physical adjustment. But he didn't get the part anyway because they got a *juvenile* juvenile. Who was ready for James Dean? – *Bill Hickey, actor*

let them dissect me like a rabbit, like a rabbit in a clinical research laboratory or something, I might not be able to produce again. They might sterilise me!'
'That man had no right to tear me down like that. You keep knocking a guy down and you'll take the guts away from him. And what's an actor without guts!' – *Jimmy Dean*

'Whatever's inside me making me what I am, it's like film. Film only works in the dark. Tear it all open and let in the light and you'll kill it.' – *Jimmy Dean*

In spite of Jimmy's resentment at the criticism he received from Strasberg, he also realised that his talent came into its own after he had met him.
'That man's a walking encyclopaedia with a fantastic insight into human behaviour. Most of what I learnt about acting comes from that man.' – *Jimmy Dean*

Another problem in those days was that the casting directors didn't think Jimmy was quite tall enough for some roles.
'How can you measure acting in inches? They're crazy.' – *Jimmy Dean*

As the work still wasn't rolling in Jimmy, together with Bill Bast and Dizzy Sheridan, was forced to live in the supreme squalor of a dingy brownstone bedsit. As always, one of their biggest preoccupations was hunger. During these lean times Jimmy would get morose and introspective and hid himself away to play his bongo drums.
'I'm playing the damn bongo and the world can go to hell.' – *Jimmy Dean*

On one particularly miserable day when he felt at the end of his tether, Jimmy suggested that they leave all their problems behind for a few days and visit his aunt and uncle's farm in Fairmount.
'Let's go to Indiana, to the farm. You'd both

Below: Dean on his first motor-cycle. Speed became an obsession – and an escape. Right: When Dean became a star the journalists searched the cuttings files for his Broadway background.

love it. It's all clean and fresh, lots of trees and open fields. Tons of good food, chicken, steak, all that jazz. We've got cows, pigs – the whole bit.' – *Jimmy Dean*

The three friends hitchhiked 800 miles to the Winslows' farm and began to unwind in the relaxed rural setting. Jimmy soon found an opportunity to show off some daredevil stunt riding tricks on his well-loved motorcycle, which had been left on the farm.
'I guess I'll never sell it. It's like a friend and brother. And friends are hard to find in the theatre.' – *Jimmy Dean*

But even in the sleepy environment of Fairmount, Jimmy's burning desire to be successful and famous was in the forefront of his mind as he considered the humdrum life of his aunt and uncle.
'Some day when I make it, I'm going to see to it that they sell this place and move to a

drier climate like Arizona where Mom's [Aunt Ortense's] arthritis won't bother her so much. Some day they're going to have the kind of life they deserve, without all the work and worry.' – *Jimmy Dean*

Their idyllic holiday was cut short when Jimmy was told by Jane Deacy to return to New York urgently, since she had an audition lined up for him in a Broadway play entitled See The Jaguar. *Before they left, Bill Bast came across his friend standing in the middle of a field in the pouring rain, shouting and gesticulating wildly – Jimmy was already preparing for his new part.*
'It teaches me to make my voice reach to the back of the theatre and also to overcome my fear of an audience.' – *Jimmy Dean*

'When Jimmy read, I was immediately taken with his qualities. He had the naiveté of a newly-hatched chick...I interviewed over a hundred young actors for that part and I was at my wits' end. I knew what I was looking for and it was a very difficult part to cast. When Dean came in, I knew he could handle the strangeness of the part.' – *Michael Gordon, director of* See The Jaguar

He was ecstatic when he got the part, especially because it afforded him the opportunity to work with well-respected theatre professionals. It also meant that he became estranged from his old friends as he threw himself completely into the part of Wally Wilkins.
'The stage is like a religion; you dedicate yourself to it and suddenly you find that you don't have time to see your friends, and it's hard for them to understand. You don't see anybody. You're all alone with your concentration and imagination and that's all you have. You're an actor.' – *Jimmy Dean*

'When he prepared an acting job, he put his heart and soul into it.' – *Bill Bast*

'I always think that my best is yet to come, and when it does arrive, I know that I shall

14. A member of Fairmount Grade School's basketball team in 1942, Jimmy (third from the right in the back row) got straight A's in art, was a popular student.

15. At 14 he clowned with cousin Marcus Winslow Jr. in the vegetable garden which was his project as a member of the local 4-H club.

20. Just graduated from high school at 18, he gets a ride from Mark Jr.

21. Right: 1950 photo of Jimmy as a theatre arts student at U.C.L.A.

16. Entering Fairmount High School, Jimmy soon proved he was a crack, all-around athlete. Posed with the baseball team in 1944 photo far left (he's second from right in back row), he also excelled as a fast basketball guard, was a champion pole vaulter.

22. Jimmy made Broadway debut in See The Jaguar, with Arthur Kennedy and Constance Ford, in 1952.

17. He was scary Frankenstein's monster in a high school comedy called Goon With The Wind.

18. President of the Thespian Society (center, at table), he played character parts in plays.

19. He won state title as a debater. His teachers knew him as brilliant but lacking application.

23. After Jaguar folded in less than a week, television roles like the one above on Danger, paid his way for two years, while he studied at the Actors' Studio.

24. TV viewers also saw him on Schlitz Playhouse, Studio One.

(Continued on next page)

JAMES DEAN ALBUM 13

12

25. Jimmy hugs co-star Geraldine Page before The Immoralist opening on Broadway in 1954.

26. As Immoralist's blackmailing Arab he won roast promising newcomer award.

27. With movie contract from Elia Kazan, he visited Winslows on way to Hollywood, played with Mark Jr.

30. On motorcycle dates his girls rode tandem seat. His hobbies, quirks and tendency to withdraw into himself made many movie-people misunderstand him.

31. Jimmy and composer Leonard Rosenman, a friend whose opera Jimmy directed at a music festival, visit set of Liberace movie together.

28. Advance raves for his performances of mixed-up farm boy in first film, East Of Eden, made him a star before its 1955 release. Next pic: Rebel Without A Cause.

29. Favorite hobby was racing sports cars. Here Jimmy accepts three trophies from Jeanne Baird for races won with a Porsche.

32. Serious Jimmy (top) studies set-design with artist Boris Levin. Below: He kids with Steffi Skolsky at 1955 party.

33. Making last movie, Giant, with Liz Taylor, Jimmy's future looked brilliant. Producers begged for his services. Then, Giant done, he set off on his last ride.

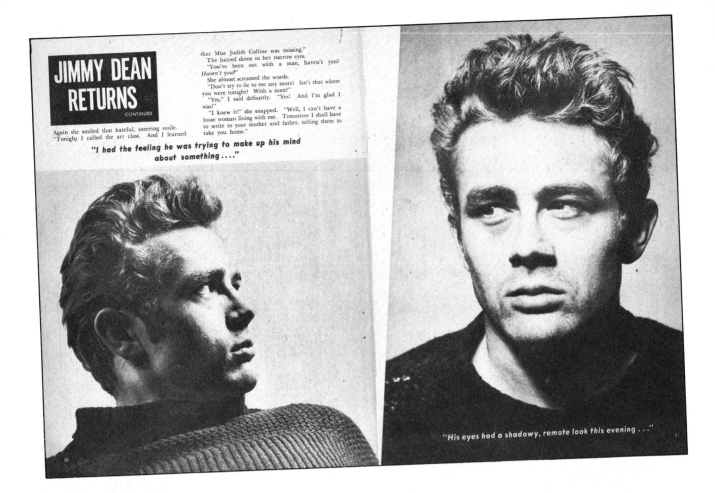

"I had the feeling he was trying to make up his mind about something...."

"His eyes had a shadowy, remote look this evening ..."

not be satisfied.' – *Jimmy Dean*

Jimmy soon fell under the influence of Michael Gordon and worked hard to impress him – both on and offstage.

'He claimed, among other things to have been a novillero in various bullrings south of the border, and I often saw him make daring passes and farinas at onrushing taxicabs while crossing Broadway or Seventh Avenue.' – *Michael Gordon*

His impetuosity and devil-may-care attitude – both qualities which were to make Jimmy such a teenage hero in his later career – were first publicly aired in a radio interview just before See The Jaguar *opened on Broadway. On being fatalistic:* 'In a certain sense I am. I don't exactly know how to explain it, but I have a hunch there are some things in life we just can't avoid. They'll happen to us, probably because we're built that way - we simply attract our own fate...make our own destiny.' – *Jimmy Dean*

'I want to live as intensely as I can. Be as useful and helpful to others as possible, for one thing. But live for myself as well. I want to feel things and experiences right down to their roots...enjoy the good in life while it is good.' – *Jimmy Dean*

Jimmy's performance on the opening night of the play on 3 December 1952 earned him a glowing review from The New York Herald Tribune. 'James Dean adds an extraordinary performance in an almost impossible role: that of a bewildered lad who has been completely shut off from a vicious world by an over-zealous mother, and who is coming upon both the beauty and brutality of the mountain for the first time.'

But the critics' overall verdict on the play was unfavourable and it closed after only six performances. However, Jimmy's talent had finally been given a proper chance to manifest itself and from then on he became far hotter property in the television casting offices. By 1953 he was

44

TV was indeed Dean's training ground – and his co-stars achieved different levels of fame. Below: Dean in a TV drama with Ronald Reagan.

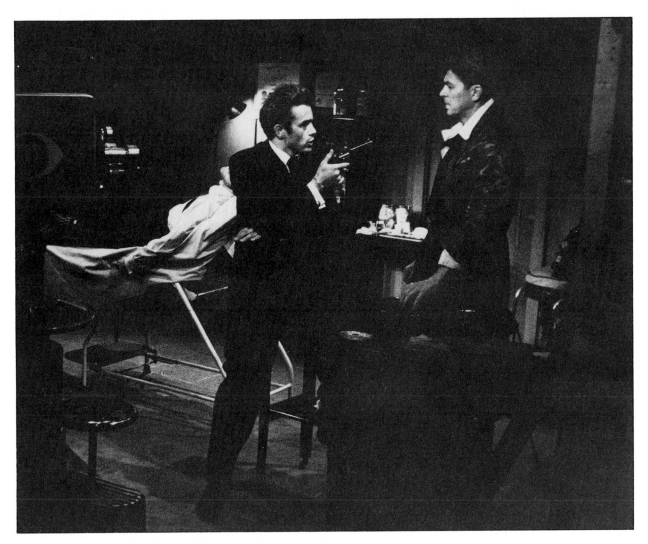

landing many young character parts and juvenile supporting roles on screen.

'I was struck by how very much James Dean off-camera resembled the James Dean you saw on-camera. He worked very hard at his craft, rehearsed with very much the same intensity that he gave the part on-camera...Most of us, after a while in pictures, hold back somewhat in rehearsal and save our punch for the take. Jimmy did not do this. He seemed to go all out almost any time that he read his lines.'
– *Ronald Reagan*

Explaining to a friend, Roy Schatt, why he was biting the tips of his fingers in order to make them more sensitive:

'Hey, you know, man, I'm doing this cowboy for TV and this guy's got to pull his gun. Got to pull his gun fast, you know. So I gotta have quick fingers.' – *Jimmy Dean*

The intensity and vigour of Jimmy's performances led inevitably to a greater number of roles which developed his aptitude for playing frustrated, vulnerable adolescents and unconventional drop-outs. Already he was attracting a devoted following of TV viewers.

'Because of his personality and because of his good looks – though being an attractive guy in itself doesn't do it – but the way Jimmy Dean presented himself was such that,

He would eat at any hour

Jimmy rehearsing for TV

He meets Kazan

WHAT HAS GONE BEFORE. In the first instalment of the James Dean Story, his friend Bill Bast told how Jimmy became seriously interested in acting. He showed that Jimmy was a restless youth, eager to improve his mind as well as his acting ability, and revealed how Jimmy decided to move to New York to pursue his acting career · · ·

LATE IN 1951, equipped with only a pocketful of change and a short list of contacts, James Dean slipped quietly out of Hollywood and headed for New York. He was off to a strange new place where he felt he would find nourishment for both his career and his mind.

The first few months in New York were mildly successful ones for Jimmy. He utilised his handful of contacts and, through them, was able to secure bit parts on radio and TV.

New York seemed to stimulate Jimmy's mind to a point where it was more alert than it had ever been. One day, during a period when he had been reading a lot of modern literature, he asked a friend to suggest something in the classic vein to read. He seemed especially interested in Greek philosophy and drama, so the friend suggested he start with Plato. That night he turned up with a volume of Plato's works and began reading a section on Democratic Education. After ... he closed the book and walked round to a bar near by. The man was a ... friend at the bar. ... than five

party at his place and a girl Jimmy knew w... her and waited downstairs in a drugstore... Brando if it would be all right to bring Jin... three hours, and finally she called. " I f... said, " until now, I just asked him." "... asked. She said, " he said no." Jimmy ... alone.

Shortly after I left New York to write for... Jimmy was cast in " The Immoralist." I ... all had gone well in the early stages of rehea... had ended badly. The out-of-town openi... a highlight, but the show to be in need o...

A new director was brought in to take ... drastically cut down. He had always sh... to any director in whom he had faith a... deliberately or unintentionally, this nev... fidence. As Jimmy related it, the direc... when he asked for guidance in his role. ... Jimmy that he left the rehearsal for severa...

Good revie...

Because of the cutting of his part ar... director, Jimmy gave his quitting notice ... in New York. In spite of the behind-... ...e show praised Jimmy's perfo...

"When Jimmy studied photography, nobody escaped his camera, not even me," Schatt says. This was at Museum of Modern Art.

PORTRAIT OF THE ACTOR IN A BIG TOWN

the photographs of
Roy Schatt

■ When young Jimmy Dean left UCLA and went East in 1953, there were only a few people who recognized in him the seeds of future greatness. One of these was Roy Schatt, the New York photographer who has shown a knack for discovering young talent long before the studios sit up and take notice. Dean spent many hours at Schatt's midtown studio, and naturally became interested in photography. Within a few months, Schatt had another full-time student on his hands. (His others have included Elia Kazan and Susan Strasberg.) "Nothing Jimmy ever did was just a sideline," Roy told us. "He put everything he was into everything he did. In his photography, he was constantly searching for the new, even the odd. Sometimes the results were bizarre. But it was always Jimmy." Roy Schatt, too, was snapping shutters as fast as he could load his cameras. Some of the candid shots he took during parties at the studio with Ji...

"Even in those days, you could sense he was troubled."
"Times like this in my studio, only the music mattered."

"And when resting, there was a part of him that r...
"Sometimes he would just stare into space, as if h...

Drinks at a roof-top restaurant

and catalogued for future reference. To James Dean, Elia Kazan was a master of his craft, a champion of his school, a maker of his destiny.

It would have been normal procedure for any good agent to submit Jimmy's name for a role in Elia Kazan's production of *East of Eden*. But Jimmy's agent—Jane Deacy—isn't merely any good agent. She is an intelligent woman with an acute eye for just the right thing, and when she read the screenplay for *Eden* she knew it was just the right thing for Dean.

So she gave Fate a gentle nudge and nursed the situation, convincing all concerned that *Eden* was the perfect vehicle for Jimmy's talent. Kazan was familiar with Jimmy's work at the Studio and had been impressed by him in " The Immoralist." He liked Jimmy and was soon convinced that he would fit the role of Cal. Jimmy was signed to do the part, then Fate stepped back to let him do the rest.

As a boy, Jimmy had had several motor-cycles. In the years away from his home in Indiana, he grew to miss the thrill, the sweet sensation of whizzing along the roads and highways. As his pocketbook fattened, he found he had enough to warrant the purchase of such a luxury.

New York is hardly the perfect place for motor-cycling, but any place will do in a pinch, and Jimmy was in a pinch. He buzzed around town from appointment to appointment, storing the cycle in the entrance-way of his apartment building when he wasn't using it. When people pointed fingers and called him " Brando-imitator," he didn't hear them. He knew what his motor-cycle meant to him—they didn't.

But, as it is so often with things you love, you get hurt by them. The week he was signed to do the role in *Eden*, Jimmy took a bad spill on the motor-cycle, scraping himself seriously. Kazan had several strong words to say about the incident and ended by instructing Jimmy to " stay off that motor-cycle." So, instead of cycling across the country to Hollywood as he had planned, Jimmy reluctantly stored the motor-cycle, packed a few things, boarded a plane, and bade farewell to New York, the city he had come to love.

As he sat on the plane his dreams of the future were strange and unnerving. But they were not nearly as fantastic as the reality into which he was speeding.

Dean set about creating a striking personal image, using the talents of photographers like Roy Schatt and Dennis Stock. The director Elia Kazan saw the new image and recognised its potential.

...ed. He seemed to be listening to something none of us could hear."

...future. He looked like he was astonished by it, but never afraid."

47

even before he really started to make it, he'd already built a cult around him, already built up people who thought very highly of Jimmy Dean.'– *Steve Ross, actor*

The fan mail began to roll in, much of it concentrating on Jimmy's physical attributes.
'You should read some of the letters from old ladies watching television. They tell me how they want me to wear tighter pants. They have this television club of ladies from 50 to 75 and they sit there checking out their cats and then write those dirty letters. It's really hard to believe.' – *Jimmy Dean*

In a department store, when the shop assistant recognised him from his television appearances:
'The last time I was in this store, nobody paid any attention to me. I was too small. All of a sudden I've grown a few inches.' – *Jimmy Dean*

At about this time, Jimmy's rebellious, unkempt

- and beautiful - image was beginning to be perfected. At a photo session with Joseph Abeles a picture appeared which finally epitomised the look Jimmy wanted to create.
'Jimmy never liked the way he looked in photographs. But when he saw this picture he looked at it and asked softly, ''Is it really *me*?'' and grabbed it and kind of hugged it to his chest.' – *Joseph Abeles*

Already Jane Deacy was looking around for the perfect first film role for Jimmy. Two roles considered were the lead in The Silver Chalice *(which eventually went to Paul Newman) and the part of Danny in* Battle Cry. *Bill Orr, the executive in charge of talent for Warner Brothers, found Jimmy's screen test a memorable experience.*
'He came in wearing these 'battle fatigues' – a dirty cap, days' worth of beard, dungarees. He was goddamned dressed for the part! And he gave the most fantastic reading I'd heard. It wasn't a reading, it was a performance! He became that character.

'I gave him the script and he looked at me and said, ''Don't just hand me this, tell me who I am.''

'So I told him, ''You're a young Polish boy being shipped off to war. You're leaving the next morning and have to say goodbye to your girlfriend and her father hates you. What do you do?''

'And he was electric! Fantastic! He would walk away with an agonised look, turn his back, then wheel quickly around and grab her. He portrayed such torment – the kind of emotion it might have taken another actor a week to do. But he didn't get the part unfortunately. Tab Hunter finally got it. He was well known and he had a contract with Warner Brothers etc. The studio finally decided it wanted a name for the picture, so Hunter was used.

'At the same time there were 100,000 people who all thought they were Marlon Brando, but Jimmy Dean wasn't one of them. If Jimmy Dean had never become what

"There was an intensity, an eagerness for life in Jimmy....It would burst out in sudden whims for scuffling and horseplay...."

JIMMY DEAN RETURNS
CONTINUED

"My folks don't live here," I told him. "They live in Ohio. They only let me come here because of Cousin Charlotte. And she—Cousin Charlotte— she has this suspicious mind, and if you came and saw her she'd tell them that—that—I don't know what she'd tell them. But she'd make them take me home again."

His voice became softer and he smiled again.
"And you don't want to go home, Judy?"
"No," I said, "I don't. Not now."
"Gee," he said, "that's the way I feel. But what are we going to do? Doesn't the old witch even let you out of the house?"

"How would it spoil everything? What can she do to you?"

18

"Of course she does," I said. "I come here to work every day and I go to art school at night."
"So how about just skipping one night of art school? Wouldn't be fatal, would it?"
I'd never thought of that. "No, it wouldn't."
"So let's make it tomorrow night, all right? I'll pick you up here after work. Okay?"
"Yes," I said.
"Swell, Judy. And if Cousin Charlotte gets suspicious—"
"I'll phone one of the other kids in the class," I said, "and find out what happened, so I can tell her."
"Great, Judy," he said. "So—till tomorrow night."
"Till tomorrow night," I said.

---

he did, I would still remember him. He was really different and left a powerful image with me.' – Bill Orr

Jimmy was disappointed that he hadn't got his break into films, but he was far from dissuaded, as he made clear in a conversation with one of his New York friends, John Gilmore.
Jimmy Dean: 'It's going to take a little longer, I know. It's going to be a little harder.'
John Gilmore: 'You know, Jimmy, you have this fixation that you're already a movie star, you really do, like it's a spiritual *fait accompli!* Only nobody else knows about it.'
Jimmy Dean: 'Yet! They don't know about it yet!'

With regular work and a certain amount of fame, Jimmy began to enjoy some of the benefits of

50

Magazine articles tried to show as many sides of Dean's character as possible – the good buddy (left), the clown (below left) and the soulful lover (below).

HIS SEARCHING HEART

With Pier Angeli, it was real love . . .

They met on the *East Of Eden* set and before long it was an open secret their commissary lunches were more than friendly meetings. Jimmy, seeking something he had lost years before, found his wordless longing answered by Pier. Then one night Pier announced this was their last date, she'd accepted Vic Damone's proposal. The day she wed, Jimmy stood across the street from the church, crying. Friends say the break-up was caused by her mother, who objected to him because he was a non-Catholic; in fact, they'd had to sneak around to see each other. Though he dated many girls after that, none replaced Pier in Jimmy's heart.

With Vampira, it was friendship.

A good deal older than Jim, Vampira first attracted him with her eccentric charms. Well-known on the west coast for her weird TV program and ghoulish costumes, she frequented Googie's Restaurant —Jimmy's favorite spot. Knowing firsthand the lonely climb up the ladder to success, she befriended him in the same way she'd befriended Marlon Brando a few years earlier. He'd go to her apartment for advice, professional and romantic —nothing more. Contrary to an article in a recent scandal magazine, which tried to paint a torrid picture of their dates, the only relationship they had was on a platonic basis.

He confided in Ursula Andress . . .

Jimmy needed advice and the 19-year-old starlet from Germany tried desperately to help him. Though they fought like cats and dogs, Jimmy admitted it was fun making up. He liked her way of telling rock bottom truth, of not taking any nonsense from him. But it was this same lack of patience on her part that made them incompatible. Ursula tried, but when she felt it wasn't working out, she switched her affections to John Derek. Moody and sullen, Jimmy dogged her footsteps for weeks afterwards, peering in car windows at her and John, confronting them at restaurants, calling her at odd hours. But he was left out in the cold.

But with Natalie Wood he had fun.

On *Rebel Without A Cause* set, Jimmy and Natalie formed a bond of friendship that gave the lie to the people who said he was peculiar and only attracted "characters." Natalie at 17, is well-adjusted, popular and well-read. They both loved to listen to records, have deep talks. But most of all they shared an intense interest in their careers. After a day of grueling shooting, they'd meet for coffee and discuss the next day's scene. For Natalie, this was not just a bobby-soxer's crush; she's much more sophisticated than that. For Dean, it could have been a chance to open the shell that always seemed to enclose him.

(Continued on next page)

being a minor star. He could afford to indulge his passion for motorbikes and moved into his own apartment on West 68th Street. He also enjoyed the flock of adoring girls who suddenly latched onto him.
'He would run into a new face and attach himself to her for a few hours, or, at the most, a day. The girls would accompany him wherever he went: to his agent's office, on interviews, to rehearsals, to dinner, on walks, or to his room.' – Bill Bast

'I got crabs, what do I do?' – Jimmy Dean

'I was cramming, like fellows used to for exams at school, only my exam was living itself! – Jimmy Dean

But a more permanent relationship began to form with Barbara Glenn, an actress whom Jimmy had met at Cromwell's Café – the favourite watering hole for aspiring actors.

'There's something so different about Jimmy. It's so hard to describe when you first meet him…the little boy quality. Insecure, uptight, but very involved. Trying desperately to make conversation, badly. I found him utterly fascinating.' – Barbara Glenn

The couple developed a very turbulent relationship, where they were always breaking up and getting back together again. Barbara was often forced to travel away from New York because of her acting, but Jimmy would write sporadically, often when he was lonely or miserable.
'I never suspected one could know as few nice people as I know. My own damn fault. Lamas and scientists may fume and quander. Everything is not just illusion. You are my proof. You have gone to Israel but you have not. I am very lonely for you. I am alone. Thoughts are sweet, then wicked,

then perverse, then penitent, then sweet. The moon is not blue. It hangs there in the sky no more.

'Please forgive me for such a sloppy letter, I'm a little drunk, drink quite a bit lately. You see, I don't know what's going on any more than you do. Remarkable lot, human beings. I care too.

'In antiphonal azure swing, souls drone their unfinished melody...When did we live and when did we not? In my drunken stupor I said a gem. I must repeat it to you, loved one. Let's see – ''Great actors are often pretentious livers. The pretentious actor, a great liver.'' (Don't get a headache over it.) God Damnit!! I miss you...You're terribly missing. Come back. Maybe I can come up and see you. You think you need understanding? Who do you think you are. I could use a little myself.'– *Jimmy Dean*

Jimmy's loneliness was in part due to the fact that Bill Bast had returned to Hollywood to write for television. On parting Jimmy warned his old friend:

'Just forget about the end results. Remember the gratification comes in the work, not in the end result. Just remember who you are and what you are, and don't take any of their guff out there.' – *Jimmy Dean*

Jimmy's new fame and fortune also meant that he no longer had to court the favour of influential people, thus increasing his reputation for being difficult and arrogant.

'The show was a *Big Story*, and I remember finding Dean rather non-communicative, showing up in old blue jeans and a checkered shirt, and he had a pair of leather gloves hanging out of his back pocket. The show was shot on location and Jimmy spent most of his time sleeping in the bus or reading Woody Woodpecker comic books. He'd slouch in his seat and his eyes would travel across the pages of Woody Woodpecker even while someone was talking to him.

Left: Dennis Stock's famous shot of Jimmy Dean as window dressing. Below: While stressing the 'lonely boy in New York' angle, 'The Real James Dean' of 1956 drew on all stages of his career.

While the director and technicians planned the planetarium scene in *Rebel*, Jimmy brooded about how he would play it.

After the shooting was finished, Jimmy, relaxed and happy with his efforts, shot the breeze with co-player Sal Mineo.

When he had a few hours off, he invariably hopped into his beloved Porsche.

Jimmy generally repaired his Porsche himself, unless the work was very difficult.

Waiting for the *Giant* cameras to roll, Jimmy flops in a folding chair in shade.

Eating in the studio commissary, Jimmy pulled his collar over his head. He was just clowning, but many people took this feeling seriously, called him anti-social and eccentric.

When the heavy equipment had been packed up, studio photographers asked Jimmy to pose for an on-the-set portrait.

With his habitual cigarette dangling from his lips, Jimmy gesticulated while chatting with a magazine photographer.

Jimmy, with the rest of the cast, complained about the amount of waiting they had to do on the location set of *Giant*.

Whitmore helped Dean decide to try his luck in New York.

The first months in Manhattan were lonely, troubled months for the sensitive Indiana farm boy. But by late 1953, his undeniable talent—newly polished at the Actors Studio—won him a good supporting part in a Broadway play, *The Immoralist*.

His performance as a "realistically unpleasant" Arab houseboy stimulated director Elia Kazan to choose him for the leading role in *East of Eden*.

Dean was the most stirring actor to hit the screen since Marlon Brando appeared in his first movie, *The Men*.

"Everything about Dean suggests the lonely, misunderstood 19-year-old," William K. Zinsser of The New York *Herald Tribune* wrote in reviewing *East of Eden*.

"When he talks, he stammers and pauses, uncertain of what he is trying to say. When he listens, he is full of restless energy—he stretches, he rolls on the ground, he chins himself on the porch railing, like a small boy impatient of his elders' chatter."

It was inevitable that Dean would be accused of imitating Brando. His defiance of Hollywood patterns of life off the screen, his employment of unconventional "realistic" actions on the screen, his abandonment of the middle voice range in favor of alternating between the mumble and the scream—all these things were reminiscent of Brando.

Dean told [*Please turn to page 62*]

'He'd been so right for the part, then here was this strange guy - like someone else had walked in after the part had been cast, someone else showing up to take Dean's part.'– *Stuart Rosenberg, TV director*

When Jimmy was told by director Archer King to stay within the chalked boundaries of the set when filming a private eye series, he exploded.
'I was trying to get a characterisation. I couldn't worry about some damn chalk mark!' – *Jimmy Dean*

In another show, Run Like A Thief, *Jimmy's eccentric and wilful behaviour antagonised other members of the cast.*
'Paul Lukas could not stand the way Dean took so much time to do his bit. At one point, Lukas had to face Diana Lynn and say, ''Excuse me, but my son [Dean] is a little peculiar.'' At dress rehearsal Dean took a great deal of time and when Lukas' turn came he said nothing. The director asked what was wrong. Lukas answered, ''I can't say my boy is peculiar; he is not peculiar. That kid is crazy.''' – *Nehemiah Persoff, actress*

Jimmy was becoming a master of the unconventional. His frustration at the rigid patterns of ordinary life was demonstrated when he moved an armchair from Cromwell's into the middle of a busy New York street and then defiantly sat in it.
'Don't you sons of bitches ever get bored? I just wanted to spark things, man, that's all. Look at you. Before I did it, we were all sitting quietly eating and drinking, and outside a lot of nine to fivers were going home to their wives, like they do every night. Now you're all juiced up, and so are they, man. They'll talk about it for years.' – *Jimmy Dean*

In one production Jimmy played a 'hep cat' killer, and for the part he had to perfect the character's jive talk. He would practise the dialect on an unsuspecting TV production assistant, Barry Shrode.

'He'd grin as he came in, wobbling his head up and down, keeping time to some unheard music like a real hep cat, which is what he was. Always ready to break down and bust some law or something, some sort of trouble that no one understood and no one knew who to blame for.

' "What's happening, man?" he'd say, always this negro jive talk. I don't know why he'd use that. I don't know what he was trying to say with it.

'He'd be on an interview or doing a show, and me, I'd want to hear what he'd been up to – I was always nibbing him about who he was in bed with. I was really partial to him, even to his sourpuss manner, those black shadows he gave off – but he'd grin and it was a lot of fun.' – *Barry Shrode*

In the late autumn of 1953 he was cast in the role of Bachir in a stage production of André Gide's novel The Immoralist. *As usual, Jimmy worked hard to explore how the character, a homosexual Arab boy, should be interpreted. He was quick to impress upon fellow actor Bill Gunn how important it was to understand and empathise with the character.*

Jimmy Dean: 'I'm in *The Immoralist.*'
Bill Gunn: 'So am I. What part are you playing?'
Jimmy Dean: 'Bachir.'
Bill Gunn: 'Hey! I'm your understudy. I'm playing this guy named somebody else and I'm also your understudy.'
Jimmy Dean: 'Oh, that's terrific! Do you know anything about Arabs?'
Bill Gunn: 'No.'
Jimmy Dean: 'Let's get into the Arabs. Let's find out what that's about.'

It is more uncertain whether Jimmy actively researched Bachir's homosexuality. When asked whether he had had homosexual experiences, he replied archly – and ambiguously:
'Well, I'm certainly not going through life with one hand tied behind my back.' – *Jimmy Dean*

'I don't know if he may have been bisexual,

you know. But I know of heterosexual activities he had in, you know, in sundry.'
– *Vampira (Maila Nurmi)*

'An actor must have a cardinal interest in all things. To interpret life you must study every aspect of it.' – *Jimmy Dean*

But the strong views he had on how to play his own part also affected the way he approached the whole play, and with some actors he gained a reputation for scene-stealing.
'Dean played every scene for himself. He tried to make improvisation of the whole damn play.' – *Paul Huber, co-actor in* The Immoralist

In a letter to Barbara Glenn, Jimmy let loose his deprecating views on the whole production.
'Rehearsals are quite confusing at this point.

Lighting, etc. Can't tell much about the show yet. Looks like a piece of shit to me. Stereophonic staging and 3-D actors. Probably be a monster success...Hate this fucking brown make-up.' – *Jimmy Dean*

But another girlfriend who Jimmy was hanging about with at the time saw a more vulnerable side to him which demonstrated his real insecurity during his preparations for the part.
'Jimmy was afraid about going into rehearsals with *The Immoralist*, he said Louis Jordan kept lifting up his nose whenever he saw Jimmy. So Jimmy made this face like an old tea maid or something, with his nose popped way up in the air. Then he'd sink down into a chair and laugh and punch the pillows. He got very depressed very easily, and a few times he'd wake me up in the middle of the night and insist that I come down to the café downstairs

56

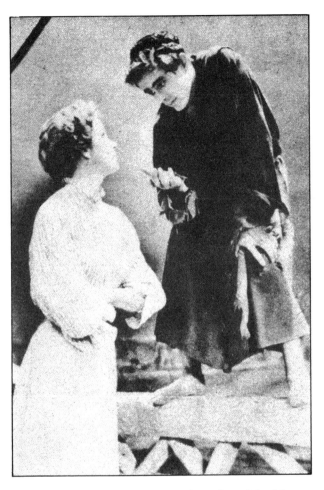

where he'd be. But it was closed and he'd know it, so he just wanted me outside with him, I guess. It was a sort of spiritual holding hands. But he would say, don't expect anything from him, or he didn't want to be ditched when the lights went out, lines like that. He'd grumble inside his jacket and everything, ''This is no good, it's no damn good,'' and his glasses fell off once and when he got them back on he said, ''Take it easy,'' and I never saw him again until we started up together in Hollywood a year later.'
– *Catherine Danian, actress*

Sparks really began to fly when, only a week before the play was due to run, the Broadway producers decided to make major changes to the script, which included cutting back Jimmy's part. The original director, Herman Schulman, with whom Dean

had struck up a good rapport, was replaced by Daniel Mann. The two men did not hit it off from the start.
'Dean was difficult to reach and totally unco-operative. In *The Immoralist* he was a destructive force. And yet, at the same time, he had flashes of real brilliance.' – *Daniel Mann*

Jimmy again wrote to Barbara:
'I am now a colourful, thieving, blackmailing Arab boy played by James Dean. Don't know who the hell I am. They are rewriting a lot. In rehearsals I was working for the elements of tragedy. A real tragedian's role, pathos etc. I turn out to be the comic relief. The Leon Errol of the show. ''Balls''.' – *Jimmy Dean*

When once Jimmy was reprimanded by Mann for not playing a scene correctly, he replied obstinately:
'I think I did all right.' – *Jimmy Dean*

'Jimmy was a tough kid to work with.' – *Adelaide Klein, actress in* The Immoralist

In spite of all the problems off-stage, Jimmy's performance at the play's première on 1 February 1954 was a triumphant success. He was given two prestigious stage awards - the Daniel Blum and Antoinette Perry (Tony) - for the most promising young actor of the year. And yet that night he quit the show. He tracked down actor Bill Hickey, telling him:
'I just wanted to tell you I quit the show. Go and get the part.' – *Jimmy Dean*

Hickey couldn't understand Jimmy's motives for leaving the play. Neither did he understand Jimmy's cryptic remark;
'I'm taken care of.' – *Jimmy Dean*

But all was soon to be revealed. Jimmy had finally won the part that was to launch him into immortality. He had been hired by the legendary Hollywood director Elia Kazan to play the lead role of Cal in his next film, East Of Eden.

Chapter 4

EAST OF EDEN

'I chose Jimmy Dean because he *was* Cal Trask. There was no point in attempting to cast it better… Jimmy was it. He had a grudge against all fathers.' Elia Kazan

Elia Kazan recognized in the real James Dean the exact combination of vulnerability and rebelliousness that he needed for the fictional Cal Trask.

Elia Kazan had been impressed by the intensity of Jimmy's acting when he saw him in The Immoralist, *and felt that this tortured, gauche young actor might be the perfect choice for the role of the adolescent misfit Cal in his new film. But Jimmy was not the only possibility. Kazan also auditioned Montgomery Clift and Paul Newman for the part, and had organised an informal screen test in which both Dean and Newman were filmed side by side. Jimmy's on-camera chemistry, which involved an awkward, pent-up aggressiveness, persuaded Kazan that this was the actor he was looking for. Jimmy's response when asked if he thought the Hollywood girls would like him was typical of his own special brand of rebelliousness which won him the part.*
'Sure. All depends on whether I like them...'
– Jimmy Dean.

Kazan was very excited about his new protégé, and explained to Montgomery Clift why he had chosen Jimmy for the part.
'He's a punk and a helluva talent, he likes racing cars, waitress – and waiters. He says you're his idol.' – Elia Kazan

But Clift already knew that he was Jimmy's idol. The young actor had contacted him by telephone to plead for a little help and encouragement.
'I'm a great actor and you're my idol and I need to see you because I need to talk to you.' – Jimmy Dean to Montgomery Clift

'Jimmy was affected by Brando, but he was more moved by Monty. Jimmy dug Monty's fractured personality – his dislocated quality. Brando was too obvious. Monty had class.' – Bill Gunn, actor

Jimmy's advance had been rejected at the time, but later Montgomery Clift was to recognise Jimmy's natural propensity to play the first American teenager.
'If I had played the James Dean character in *East Of Eden*, the part would have come out as a maladjusted neurotic, instead of a mixed-up boy.' – Montgomery Clift

60

The only film to be released during his lifetime, 'East of Eden' continued to make an impact with fifties teenagers after his death, as this 'Screen Stories' feature of 1955 shows.

HE WAS CRUEL AND WILD BECAUSE HE KNEW HIS FATHER HATED HIM . . . THE STORY OF A BOY'S SEARCH FOR LOVE.

EAST of EDEN

JAMES DEAN
•
JULIE HARRIS

They were brothers, all right, born of the same parents—but anyone who knew Cal and Aron Trask found it hard to believe. Even their father did. To Adam Trask, whose wife had left him right after the second son was born, his boys were as different as night and day. Aron, at twenty-three, was reliable and cooperative and a devoted son. Not so twenty-one-year-old Cal. Here was a wild one, moody and quick to anger, clearly destined for trouble. His father said he was bad

(Continued on page 50)

"I know love is beautiful and good," Abra (Julie Harris) had whispered to Cal (James Dean), but she was afraid of her feelings for him.

PRAISE FOR A YOUNG MAN'S GREATNESS

Screen Stories, Oct., 1955

So it was that in spring 1954 Jimmy packed his bags and left with Kazan for Hollywood – and a life which would elevate him onto a totally different plane.

'I took Jimmy out to California. He hadn't been there since he was a kid. I picked him up in a car and he had his clothes in a paper bag. He'd never been in an airplane before. He kept looking down over the side of the fucking plane, just watching the ground. He was totally innocent. It was all new to him.' – Elia Kazan

When he got to California, Jimmy started preparing for his part. In the film, Caleb Trask is the proverbial black sheep of the family, and the film focusses on the tensions which ensue between Cal and his puritanical father, his squeaky-clean brother and a mother who long ago abandoned her family for the life of a brothel-keeper. The story of the film in many ways reflected Jimmy's own turbulent childhood.

'I chose Jimmy Dean because he *was* Cal Trask. There was no point in attempting to cast it better or nicer. Jimmy was it. He had a grudge against all fathers. He was vengeful; he had a sense of aloneness and being persecuted. And he was suspicious.' – Elia Kazan

Jimmy also felt that most of the preparation for the part was already under his belt.

61

'I didn't read the novel. The way I work, I'd much rather justify myself with the adaptation rather than the source. I felt I wouldn't have any trouble – too much anyway – with this characterisation once we started because I think I understood the part. I knew, too, that if I had any problems over the boy's background, I could straighten it out with Kazan.' – *Jimmy Dean*

Although Jimmy perfectly fitted his role emotionally, Kazan felt that his scrawny, downbeat appearance needed to be improved upon in order to create the perfect image of a country farmboy.
'Kazan sent Jimmy to the desert to get a suntan and made him drink a pint of cream a day. It was kind of ironic to fatten him up to make him look like a farmboy, because he was a farmboy. He had that lean look from doing it. And suddenly he had this rubber tyre. And this suntan. I'd never seen him suntanned! But this was Kazan's conception

of the farmboy. Healthy. Fat. Cornfed. I think he got the pigs mixed up with the farmers.
'Jimmy hated it. They cut his hair, fattened him up, put make-up on him, all this stuff. Maybe to make up for the fact that he wasn't six foot.' – *Bill Gunn, actor*

Although Jimmy would compromise with the great and talented Elia Kazan on such matters, his attitude to the Hollywood system in general was distrustful and defensive because of the humiliating memories of his earlier failures. He told Bill Bast:
'They gave me a lot of guff out here last time. They're not going to do it again. This time I'm going to make sure of it.' – *Jimmy Dean*

Or as Jimmy's friend Vivian Coleman put it:
'Jimmy didn't go back to Hollywood with a chip on his shoulder, it was a boulder.'

'Why the hell must I change? No bastard's

Left: One of Dennis Stock's Fairmount series of pictures, the only publicity session Dean agreed to before the opening of 'East of Eden'. Right: Brotherly alienation – James Dean and Richard Davalos as the Trask brothers.

we're in the middle of a conference. Haven't you got any manners?' – *Jimmy Dean*

After the agent had left, Jimmy explained that he had an old vendetta against him from his previous time in Hollywood.
'That loud-mouthed slob. Four years ago he gave me a hard time on an interview here.' – *Jimmy Dean.*

But Jimmy's volatile image was somewhat encouraged by Warners – the film company Jimmy was signed to – because they wanted to groom their latest 'find' to appeal to a younger, more restless generation of moviegoers. His first press release was not a string of publicity clichés, but contained surprising statements which admitted both to his unglamorous, boy-next-door background and to his neurotic nature.
'Cows, pigs, chickens and horses may not appear to be first-rate dramatic coaches, but believe it or not I learned a lot about acting from them. Working on a farm gave me an insight on life, which has been of tremendous help to me in my character portrayals...A neurotic person has the necessity to express himself and my neuroticism manifests itself in the dramatic. Why do most actors act? To express the fantasies in which they have involved themselves.' – *Jimmy Dean, in his first press release*

telling me what to do. Everything I've done has been done on my own terms. I'll take orders from no one.' – *Jimmy Dean*

Jimmy's surly and uncompromising attitude towards the Hollywood system manifested itself from day one. After all he now had the upper hand, since he was finally in demand.
'I don't need Hollywood. Maybe they don't need me either, but I've got the advantage. I've got something they want and they're going to have to pay to get it.' – *Jimmy Dean*

When he met his Hollywood agent, Dick Clayton, for the first time Jimmy was out to prove in no uncertain terms that he was going to play it his way. When his meeting with Dick was interrupted by another agent, Jimmy let fly.
'You come in here, braying like an ass when

When filming actually started, Jimmy moved into an apartment with Dick Davalos who played his screen brother, Aron. The tension Kazan had intended to create by this intimate living arrangement soon manifested itself on the set – and on the screen.
'During *East of Eden* Jimmy and I shared a one-room apartment over the drugstore across the street from Warner Brothers. And we were Aron and Cal to the teeth. It crept into our social life. He would do something and I would reject him, and he would follow me down the street twenty paces behind. I went through many numbers, baby, but it was worth it.' – *Dick Davalos*

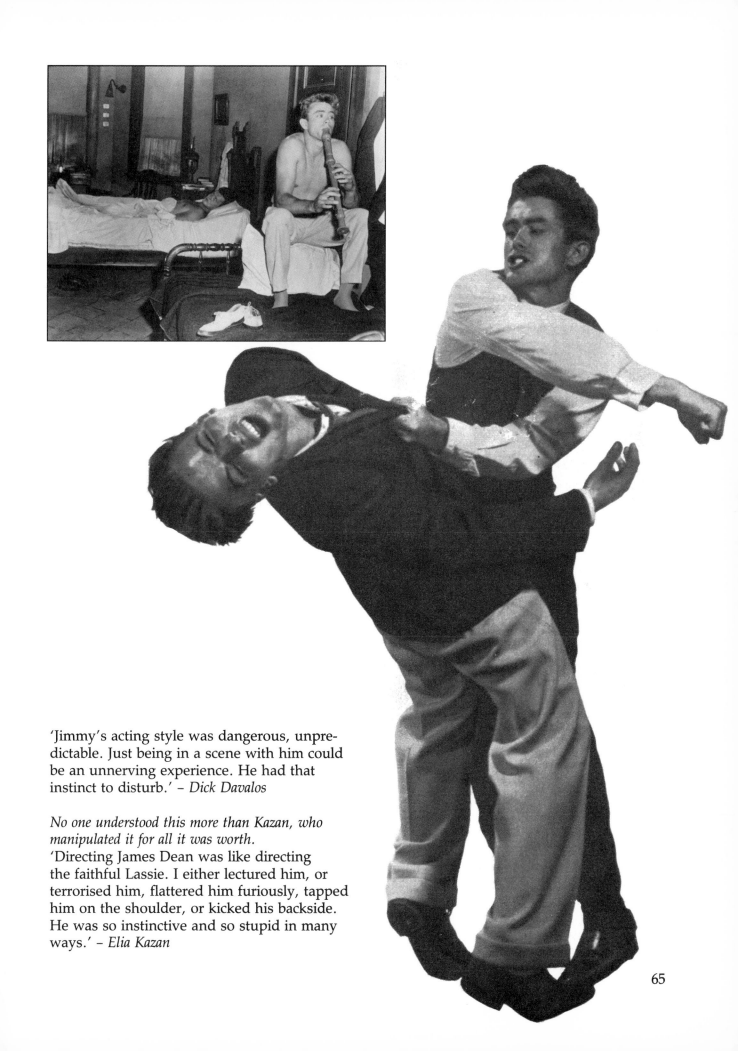

'Jimmy's acting style was dangerous, unpre-
dictable. Just being in a scene with him could
be an unnerving experience. He had that
instinct to disturb.' – *Dick Davalos*

*No one understood this more than Kazan, who
manipulated it for all it was worth.*
'Directing James Dean was like directing
the faithful Lassie. I either lectured him, or
terrorised him, flattered him furiously, tapped
him on the shoulder, or kicked his backside.
He was so instinctive and so stupid in many
ways.' – *Elia Kazan*

65

Many of the youthful pronouncements made by Jimmy Dean while still trying to make a name for himself were seized upon by the memorial albums and examined minutely, as in this 'James Dean Album' of 1956.

THE REAL JIMMY DEAN

In dance class with Eartha Kitt, he was a willing, if awkward, pupil. Other enthusiasms reflected in his apartment were bull-fighting, reading and bongo drums which he even took home to the farm.

For Jim, life was a quest and his goal was

James Dean once said, "If I live to be a hundred, there won't be time to do everything I want." Sadly he did not live even one quarter of that time and of all the dreams that died with him perhaps the greatest was his life-long dream of finding himself.

It is no secret that there were many in Hollywood who did not understand, and therefore did not like, Jimmy. They considered his awkward withdrawal a kind of snobbishness, his inability to communicate, deliberate rudeness. In his relations with the press,

to find himself. How well did he succeed?

he was particularly unfortunate. He did not feel that what he ate for breakfast or what he wore to bed had any bearing on his stature as an artist and he avoided the reporters who asked these questions.

Similarly he ran from those who posed deeper, more philosophical queries, for in all honesty he did not always know the answers himself.

How did he act? Why did he act? Where was he going from here? When Dean streaked across the screen in *East Of Eden*, there was a tendency to brush off his genius with a *(Continued on next page)*

BY ALICE PACKARD

'The serious artist has always been misunderstood.' – *Jimmy Dean*

Jimmy, who could never really handle criticism, was lucky to have actress Julie Harris on the set to counteract Kazan's tyrannical manipulations. Julie Harris, who played Aron's girlfriend in the film, would coax and encourage him to find his best. She also provided a shoulder to cry on for a boy who was still disorientated by the pressures and pitfalls of Hollywood.
'He was desperately lonely and had many inward problems so it was hard to get close to him. He was a strange and sensitive character with tremendous imagination.' – *Julie Harris*

Jimmy wrote of this loneliness to his old girlfriend back in New York, Barbara Glenn.
'I don't like it here. I don't like people here. I like it home (N.Y.) and I like you and I want to see you. Must I always be miserable? I try so hard to make people reject me. Why? I don't want to write this letter. It would be better to remain silent. Wow! Am I fucked up...I WANT TO DIE. I have told the girls here to kiss my ass and what sterile, spineless prostitutes they were. I HAVEN'T BEEN TO BED WITH NOBODY. And won't until after the picture and I am home safe in N.Y.C. (snuggly little town that it is) sounds unbelievable but it's the truth I swear. So hold everything, stop breathing, stop the town all of N.Y.C. until (should have trumpets here) James Dean returns. Wow! Am I fucked up. I got no motorcycle I got no girl.' – *Jimmy Dean*

But it didn't take long to remedy this sorry state of affairs. Jimmy was soon cruising round Hollywood in a red MG sports car and was seen dating a string of pretty young starlets. Many of these dates were set up by the studio as good

Jimmy chats to Julie Harris (seated), Richard Davalos (left) and other members of the 'East of Eden' crew during a break in shooting. Below: Magazines like 'The Real James Dean' stressed Jimmy as a loner, on and off screen.

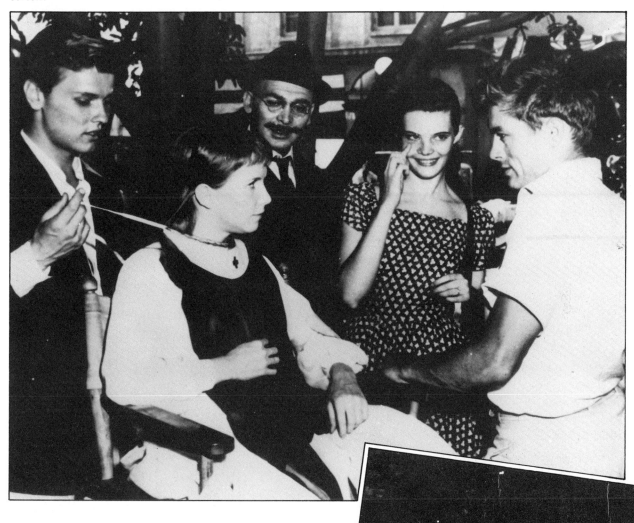

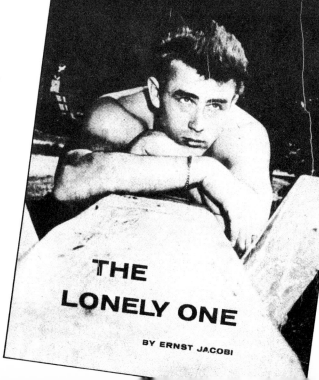

THE
LONELY ONE

BY ERNST JACOBI

publicity for their new rising star, but Jimmy's naturally curious nature soon led him to look beyond Warners' list of eligible romantic fodder. One of his first female acquaintances was Vampira – a TV personality who cultivated a spooky, rather satanic image and who was considered to be 'hip'. But Jimmy was soon bored by her superficiality. 'I have never taken Vampira out, and I should like to clear this up. I have a fairly adequate knowledge of satanic forces, and I was interested to find out if this girl was obsessed by such a force. She was a subject about which I wanted to learn. I met her and engaged her in conversation. She knew absolutely nothing! She uses her characterisation as an excuse for the most

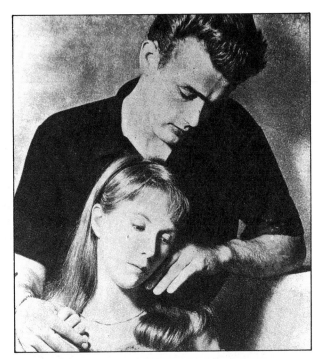

infantile expression you can imagine.' – *Jimmy Dean*

Jimmy's interest in Vampira's satanic image must in part have been linked with his role as Cal in East Of Eden *– a role which explored the destructive and hostile elements of human nature.* 'I can't divert into being a social human being when I've been working on a hero like Cal, who's essentially demonic.' – *Jimmy Dean*

Jimmy had met Ella Logan, a friend of Kazan's, on the set of Eden, *and his fascination with the evil side of human nature was revealed to her.* 'I like you, Ella. You're good. But, you know, I like bad people, too. I guess that's because I'm curious to know what makes them bad.' – *Jimmy Dean.*

In response to the enduring myth of the neurotic outsider, fifties memorabilia such as this 'James Dean Anniversary Book' constantly emphasised the tragic side of Dean's character.

melancholy genius

The Life Story of James Dean:

■ When *East of Eden* opened in New York last winter— replete with tickets selling for $150 each for the benefit of the Actors' Studio, and celebrity-ushers in snappy uniforms to lead the celebrities to their seats—the man who created the greatest stir was someone who wasn't there: James Dean. Studio representatives tore their hair in private, smiled sweetly in public, and admitted both privately and publicly that Jimmy had been brought to New York expressly to make friends and influence the press, but they hadn't the slightest notion of where he was.

While Warners' New York office kept the telephone wires humming all that week in a vain effort to track him down for the dozens of newspapermen and magazine writers who wanted to interview him, Jimmy spent a quiet week in New York virtually in hiding—visiting friends at the Actors' Studio, where he'd once been a student, taking in the shows, and catching up on fun he'd missed with old friends Bill Gunn, the Negro actor who appeared on Broadway in *Take A Giant Step*, and Marty Landau, a TV actor. The three of them sauntered past the Astor one day, and stood quietly gazing up at the marquee with Jimmy's name emblazoned in lights on it: just looking up at it with the proper amount of awe. When Jimmy spotted the manager (who was wearing a full-dress suit in broad daylight, as theatre managers do) the triumvirate slinked off as though they'd been trespassing on an estate that said "keep out" and had been caught.

His behavior may have astonished the studio and astounded reporters, but it needn't have. On the record, Jimmy's friends will tell you that he doesn't go for those after-the-show congratulations, that he doesn't think they're sincere. But off the record, they'll admit that "he's probably the most sensitive guy in the world" and allergic to both criticism and praise. Big crowds frighten him. Strangers asking personal questions make him ill at ease. He's been labeled anti-social by some, rebellious by others, and just plain shy by those who think they understand him—but he's attracted some very loyal friends. And Hollywood, viewing the sets closed to visitors, the motorcycle, the sneakers, and the complete disregard for publicity, calls him "another Marlon Brando" and lets it go at that.

Jimmy counters that "People were telling me I behaved like Brando before I knew who Brando was. I'm not disturbed by the comparison, nor am I flattered." (To which Louis Sobol wryly added the aside, "Dear boy, neither is Brando.") By way of dismissing the subject for all time, Jimmy adds succinctly, "I have my own personal rebellion and don't have to rely on Brando's."

That should be that. But it isn't. Jimmy Dean is an actor who creates controversy—and perhaps a little of the riddle of his complex behavior is to be explained rather simply in terms of his past, and the fact that he was uprooted from a happy home before he was able to cope with it.

Jimmy was the only child of Winton and Mildred Dean, an Indiana couple who'd met, courted and married not far from Mario, Indiana, and who had moved to the West Coast when Winton Dean got a job as a dental technician in a hospital there. When Jimmy was 9, his mother died suddenly of an incurable disease. Jimmy's father had known that Mrs. Dean's death was imminent, and tried to comfort the youngster despite his own bereavement and loss. "I tried to prepare him, to make him understand," Jim's father declares. "But I just couldn't get through to the boy." Death, which sometimes brings people closer together than before, succeeded only in adding mileage to the emotional distance between Jim and his Dad. Mr. Dean, feeling that he might not be able to give little Jimmy the love and affection he needed, sent him off to Indiana to live with his aunt and uncle. Robbed of his father as well as his mother, Jim discovered very early in life what it meant to be lonely....

(Continued on page 61)

HE CARRIED HIS DOOM LIKE A BANNER

Hollywood Life Stories, 1955

But much of Cal's hostility and aggression was already inherent in Jimmy's character.
'The picture is a study in dualities – that it is necessary to arrive at goodness through a sense of the satanic rather than the puritanic...I considered it a great challenge to reveal honestly the things in my part that were of myself as well as the character. I hate anything that limits progress or growth. I hate institutions that do this; a way of acting, a way of thinking.' – *Jimmy Dean*

An attitude such as this jarred with many of the characters and crew involved in the film. One of the first people to fall out with Jimmy was Raymond Massey, who played Cal's father. In a scene where Cal is forced by his father to read from the Bible as a punishment for wilfully destroying blocks of ice, Jimmy antagonised Massey by substituting four-letter words for the actual psalm he was supposed to read. This resulted in a furious outburst by Massey – a reaction which was exactly what Kazan had wanted to catch on film. But Jimmy wouldn't always save his churlish behaviour for the dramatic parts of the film. Eventually most of the cast, including Kazan himself, were disaffected with Jimmy.

'When we first worked together we became close friends, but as time went on he became more neurotic, he turned against me, he was a very troubled person.' – *Elia Kazan*

'I'm a serious-minded and intense little devil, terrible gauche and so tense I don't see how people stay in the same room with me. I know I wouldn't tolerate myself.' – *Jimmy Dean*

Jimmy Dean is in "East of Eden" and "Rebel Without a Cause"

Demon Dean

Out of the corner
of his eyes he's daring
Hollywood to change him.
And telling the world
in his bebop lingo, he means
to act, not charm!

BY SIDNEY SKOLSKY

● Scene: Early in the morning at Googie's. A low-priced restaurant.
The young crowd gather here after Schwab's (next door) cl——
at midnight. I'm sitting with a group in the booth in the——
Between coffee and hot cakes and hot chocolate——
about acting. Then a young fellow approac——
a black leather jacket, a pair of old ——
Jimmy Dean. I can tell by th——
him. The talk continues——
his mouth. When ——
like this: "——
them ——

38

24

Take a good look at James Dean. He
dresses—and behaves—like Brando.
He admits he's a "devil" and can't
see how people manage to stay in
the same room with him. Yet . . .

You Can't Ignore the New Scowl Boy

SAYS DONOVAN PEDELTY

IN the forest of words already written about this
gangling, twenty-four year old Indiana farm boy who
has gone Big Time, the most outspoken comment
comes from a New York critic. Of James Dean he
writes: "His eye is as empty as an animal's,"

He comes, says the critic I have just quoted, from the
"tilted school of naturalistic actin——otherwise known
as the Actors' Studio of New ——by (in)
Kazan, director of "East Of E——
who also taught and directed M——
Dean, with his blue jeans and
shirt for party wear, his roar-
ing motor-cycle, his morose
moods, his refusal for sometimes four days on end to answer the phone, has been
accused of doing a Brando."

But Brando gives the impression on the screen of being
a profound and important
human being, however puzzled.
To me, Dean rapidly becomes
rather tiring.

In East Of Eden, Dean, as
an unloved son, flings himself
about in every direction to
secure the attention—yours and
mine, as picturegoers.

Controversial

Off-screen, he has a talent
for being controversial. The
motor-cycle and dirty shirt
style has been done before,
not better, perhaps, but more
originally by Brando. So have
the moods, the scowls and the
unanswered phone.

It is amusing that as Dean
picked up the T-shirt rôle
Brando dropped it. At the
last party they both attended,
Marlon—in his own closed car
——came in impeccably cut dark
——it——with tab-collared
——shirt and
——Homburg hat

Give own
in his own ——
"Both Bra——
from farms, we ——
please, ride motor-c——
work for Elia Kaza——
actor, I have no ——
behave like B——
don't attempt to ——
"Nevertheless, ——
difficult not to ——
not to carry a ——
highly success——
is, so to speak ——
school. ——
"I find, h——
more I wor——
the tendenc——
Brandoism ——
On the ——
turned fro——
acting: "I——
became——
person ——
expres——
neuro——
it in th——

"There
used t
He

70

Magazines like 'Photoplay' (top) and 'Picturegoer' (below) leapt at the chance of promoting the image of the wild boy which the 'East of Eden' publicity machine was feeding them at the time of the film's release.

'He got kind of spoiled, abusing, throwing his weight around.' – *Elia Kazan*

This was manifested most strikingly in Jimmy's behaviour towards the press. The Hollywood publicity machine encouraged hounding reporters to reveal the most trivial and mindless details in the lives of its screen gods and goddesses. And of course the Hollywood deities were expected to cooperate – an obligation which Jimmy was determined not to fulfil.
'I came to Hollywood to act, not to charm society. The objective artist has always been misunderstood. I probably should have a press agent. But I don't care what people write about me. I'll talk to reporters I like, the others can print whatever they please.' – *Jimmy Dean*

'Maybe publicity is important, but I just can't make it, can't get with it. I've been told by a lot of guys the way it works. The newpapers give you a big build-up. Something happens, they tear you down. Who needs it? What counts to the artist is performance not publicity. Guys who don't know me, already they've typed me as an oddball.' – *Jimmy Dean*

Jimmy's uncompromising attitude immediately alienated most of the Hollywood reporters, among them the influential columnist Hedda Hopper, who remembered vividly her first meeting with him.
'The latest genius sauntered in, dressed like a bum, and slouched down in silence at a table away from mine. He hooked another chair with his toe, dragged it close enough to put his feet up, while he watched me from the corner of his eye. Then he stood up to inspect the framed photographs of Warner stars that covered the wall by his head. He chose one of them, spat in its eye, wiped off his spittle with a handkerchief, then like a ravenous hyena, started to gulp the food that had been served him.
' ''Would you like to meet him?'' said the

Below and right: Jimmy Dean with Pier Angeli, probably the only woman he really loved. Even so he drove her away, providing 'Top Spot' with a ready-made plot for a picture story (below right).

studio press agent who was my escort.

' ''No thank you, I've seen enough. If that's your prize package, you can take him. I don't want him.'' ' – *Hedda Hopper*

It was at about this time that Jimmy also managed to alienate the most precious person he had met whilst in Hollywood – Pier Angeli. Pier was an Italian-born actress whom he had met on the set of The Silver Chalice, *which was being filmed next to* East Of Eden. *He was hypnotised by her Latin charm and grace.*
'Foreign girls intrigue me.' – *Jimmy Dean*

Jimmy immediately fell for her demure, reflective nature and the feeling was reciprocated. The couple were soon lovers.
'Pier's a rare girl, I respect her. Unlike most Hollywood girls, she's real and genuine.' – *Jimmy Dean*

'He is a wonderful boy, a great actor.' – *Pier Angeli*

'I can talk to her. She understands.' – *Jimmy Dean*

'Jimmy is different, he loves music. He loves it from the heart the way I do. We have so much to talk about. It's wonderful to have such understanding.' – *Pier Angeli*

'Her soul, she's got a beautiful soul. Strikes you right away. Beauty. Sheer overwhelming beauty.' – *Jimmy Dean*

The couple were soon seeing a lot of each other. But their relationship steered away from the usual Hollywood formula of glamorous dinner dates and film previews towards a greater intimacy and spontaneity.

72

But it was a romance doomed before it had begun. The studio didn't like it for publicity and fan-interest reasons ; Pier's mother opposed it on religious grounds. Dean was on the losing end : a few months later, Pier married Vic Damone.

THEY SAY THAT AS THE GUESTS LEFT THE CHURCH THEY SAW A MAN IN BLACK REV UP A MOTOR CYCLE ENGINE, AND RIDE FURIOUSLY AWAY.

IT WAS DEAN. DISAPPOINTED AND BITTER HE RODE TO FAIRMOUNT AND SHUT HIMSELF AWAY FOR THREE DAYS.

HE WENT BACK TO WORK, MORE MOROSE THAN EVER. HE TRIED TO REPLACE HIS BROKEN ROMANCE WITH A LOVE FOR FAST CARS. HE WENT IN FOR RACING, AND WON TROPHIES.

HE MET A LOVELY STARLET BY THE NAME OF LORI NELSON.

THEY WENT RIDING . . .

HE MADE ANOTHER PICTURE—"REBEL WITHOUT A CAUSE". NOW THE TEENAGERS WENT REALLY WILD ABOUT HIM. HIS SUCCESS WAS FABULOUS.

BUT DEAN WAS HARD TO LIVE WITH. HIS BROKEN ROMANCE HAD ENLARGED THE IMAGINARY CHIP ON HIS SHOULDER. HE JUST SEEMED ANGRY AT EVER HAVING BEEN BORN. HE HURT HIS FRIENDS BY HIS SLOVENLINESS, HIS RUDENESS AND BY HIS BEHAVIOR IN PRIVATE LIFE.

73

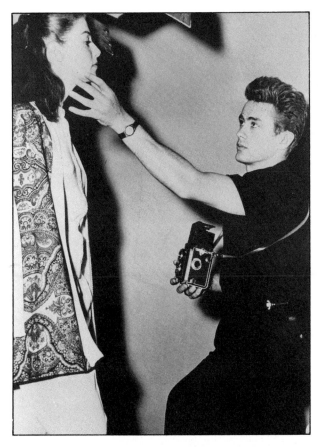

it. We saw a great deal of each other when we weren't making films. We were young and wanted to enjoy life together and we did. Sometimes we would just drive along and stop at a hamburger stand for a meal or go to a drive-in movie. It was all so innocent and emphatic.' – *Pier Angeli*

But he failed to understand her family, who were strict Catholics and who intended to preserve Pier's madonna-like persona. Pier's mother was outraged at Jimmy's lack of respect for their Italian way of life, especially when she received this surly reply to her complaint that in Rome boyfriends would not dream of bringing her daughter home as late as Jimmy did:
'When in Rome, do as the Romans do. Welcome to Hollywood.' – *Jimmy Dean*

No one seemed to approve of the match, neither Pier's parents, her film studio or Jimmy's trusted friend and agent, Jane Deacy, who warned him:
'If you marry her, you'll be Mr Pier Angeli.' – *Jane Deacy*

Jimmy was in a state of confusion and apprehension about the future of their relationship. When asked by a friend if he would be marrying Pier, he answered:
'You mean with Miss Pizza? Look, I'm just too neurotic, but I mean who knows, am I right?' – *Jimmy Dean*

'She's an untouchable. We're members of totally different castes. She's the kind of girl you put on a shelf and look at. Anyway, her old lady doesn't dig me. Can't say I blame her.' – *Jimmy Dean*

'I wouldn't marry her unless I could take care of her properly. And I don't think I'm emotionally stable enough to do so right now.'– *Jimmy Dean*

But to Pier herself Jimmy made equivocal promises.
'We'll work something out...But we won't get

'We used to go together to the California coast and stay there secretly in a cottage on a beach far away from prying eyes. We'd spend much of our time on the beach, sitting there or fooling around, just like college kids. We would talk about ourselves and our problems, about the movies and acting, about life and after death. Sometimes we would just go for a walk along the beach, not actually speaking, but communicating our love silently to each other. We had complete understanding of each other.

'We were like Romeo and Juliet, together and inseparable. Sometimes on the beach we loved each other so much we just wanted to walk together into the sea holding hands because we knew then that we would always be together. It wasn't that we wanted to commit suicide. We loved our life, and it was just that we wanted to be close to each other always.

'We didn't need to be seen together at film premières or night clubs. We didn't need to be in gossip columns or be seen at the big Hollywood parties. We were like kids together and that's the way we both liked

Below: After the release of 'East of Eden' the 'Film Show Annual' devoted a feature to Dean.

Spotlighting **JAMES DEAN** Warner Bros. new sensational star, answers some personal questions for Film Show Annual readers

JAMES DEAN is my real name. *Height?* 5 feet 10 inches . . . *Weight?* 155 pounds . . . . *Colour of eyes?* Blue . . . *Hair?* Blond . . . *Nationality?* American . . . *Where were you born?* Fairmount, Indiana . . . *Date of Birth?* February 8, 1931. . . . *What schools did you attend?* Grammar and High School in Fairmount. *College?* University of California at Los Angeles. *In what school sports did you participate?* Baseball, track, basketball. *Did you take part in school dramatics?* Yes. *Were any of your relatives theatrical people?* No. *Who brought you up?* My uncle and aunt, as my mother died while I was a baby. *When did you start acting?* In High School. *To whom do you give credit for stimulating your interest in acting?* To James Whitmore,

who lived near the university in Los Angeles. We had many serious talks. I was taking a pre-law course then. *Did you finish your course in law?* No. I left the campus after two years. I decided I wanted to be a professional actor. I headed for New York. *What was your first stage role?* I played the role of a boy who has been shut in an ice house for ten years in " See the Jaguar ". *What was your next important role?* The blackmailing Arab in " The Immoralist ". *How did you happen to go on the screen?* Elia Kazan saw me in " The Immoralist " and decided to test me for *East of Eden*, the film he was about to produce and direct at Warner Bros. in Hollywood. *List the pictures in which you have appeared?* East of Eden, Rebel Without a Cause, and Giant. *What arts are you most interested in outside of acting?* Sailing, fencing, gymnastics, boxing, tennis, and an academic interest in bullfighting. *What is your pet aversion?* Nightclubs. *What extravagances do you have?* I buy a lot of camera equipment, buy lots of records, and keep a palomino horse. *What is your taste in books?* I like books that are on the serious side. I read everything from books on culture, expressionistic literature, and philosophical works. Sometimes I read six at a time, skipping from book to book—generally managing to get them all read at about the same time. *Are you orderly?* No—I'm told that stepping into my house is like arriving at the scene of a hurricane. My belongings are strewn everywhere, in my home in the Hollywood hills. I am not always in a rush! When I don't have a call to work early on a studio set I prefer to stay up late and then try to sleep till almost noon. Unless I absolutely have to dress up off-screen, I would rather jump into old dungarees and a T-shirt. *What sort of girls do you date?* Usually actresses, so that we can talk more about the screen, stage and television. I don't think I am self-centred, because I am very concerned with the hopes and problems of others. In New York I sometimes took girl friends out on the rear seat of my motor-cycle. In Hollywood I have a little foreign car now and am happy to share it with my real friends.

61

married.' – *Jimmy Dean*

The pressures which were plaguing his romance with Pier Angeli began to make Jimmy feel depressed and moody. He wrote to Barabara Glenn in New York.
'Have been very dejected and moody last two weeks. Have been telling everybody to fuck off and that's no good. I could never make them believe I was working on my part. Poor Julie Harris doesn't know what to do with me. Well to hell with her, she doesn't have to do anything with me. Everyone turns into an idiot out here. I have only one friend, one guy that I can talk to and be understood. I hope Lennie comes out here. I need someone from New York. Cause I'm mean and I'm really kind and gentle. Things get mixed up

all the time. I see a person I would like to be close to (everybody) then I think it would be just the same as before and they don't give a shit for me. Then I say something nasty or nothing at all and walk away. The poor person doesn't know what's happened. He doesn't realise that I have decided I don't like him. What's wrong with people. Idiots.' – *Jimmy Dean*

Elia Kazan recognised that Jimmy's turbulent affair with Pier could have catastrophic results for East Of Eden, *which was in its last few weeks of filming.*
'He got into something with Pier Angeli and got very upset. He had an uncertain relationship with women. He got upset and it was affecting his work, so since I was alone

After his death Jimmy Dean's films were endlessly featured in the press, almost shot by shot, as the only permanent legacy of his work.

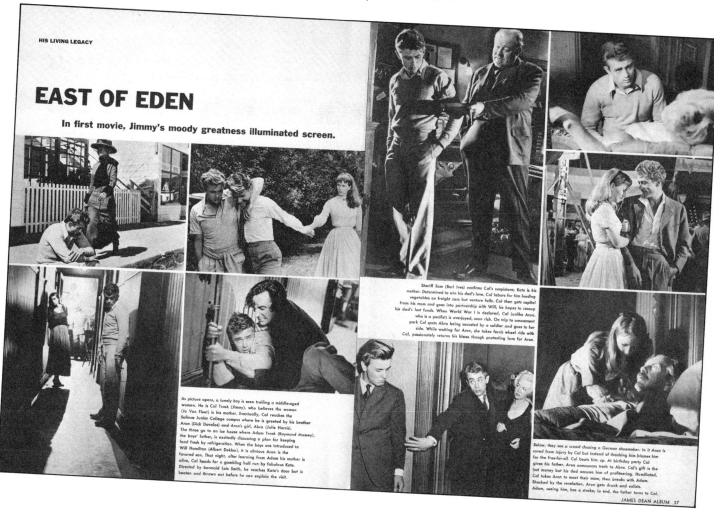

EAST OF EDEN

In first movie, Jimmy's moody greatness illuminated screen.

As picture opens, a lonely boy is seen trailing a middle-aged woman. He is Cal Trask (Jimmy), who believes the woman (Jo Van Fleet) is his mother. Eventually, Cal reaches the Salinas Junior College campus where he is greeted by his brother Aron (Dick Davalos) and Aron's girl, Abra (Julie Harris). The three go to an ice house where Adam Trask (Raymond Massey), the boys' father, is excitedly discussing a plan for keeping food fresh by refrigeration. When the boys are introduced to Will Hamilton (Albert Dekker), it is obvious Aron is the favored son. That night, after learning from Adam his mother is alive, Cal heads for a gambling hall run by fabulous Kate. Directed by barmaid Lois Smith, he reaches Kate's door but is beaten and thrown out before he can explain the visit.

Sheriff Sam (Burl Ives) confirms Cal's suspicions: Kate is his mother. Determined to win his dad's love, Cal labors for him loading vegetables on freight cars but venture fails. Cal then gets capital from his mom and goes into partnership with Will; he hopes to recoup his dad's lost funds. When World War I is declared, Cal (unlike Aron, who is a pacifist) is overjoyed, soon rich. On trip to amusement park Cal spots Abra being accosted by a soldier and goes to her side. While waiting for Aron, she takes ferris wheel ride with Cal, passionately returns his kisses though protesting love for Aron.

Below, they see a crowd chasing a German shoemaker. In it Aron is saved from injury by Cal but instead of thanking him blames him for the free-for-all. Cal beats him up. At birthday party Cal gives his father, Aron announces troth to Abra. Cal's gift is the lost money but his dad accuses him of profiteering. Humiliated, Cal takes Aron to meet their mom, then breaks with Adam. Shocked by the revelation, Aron gets drunk and enlists. Adam, seeing him, has a stroke; in end, the father turns to Cal.

JAMES DEAN ALBUM 27

– my wife wasn't there – I told him I'm going to live in the dressing room, I don't want to live in the hotel any more. I got into the dressing room next to him and we both lived in adjoining dressing rooms on the lot...so I kept my eye on him night and day, so we'd be sure to get through the goddam picture.' – *Elia Kazan*

By the middle of August, Eden was completed, and Jimmy had to be thrown out of his dressing room in the Warner lot where he was still living, since it was company policy not to allow actors to 'live in'.

'After *East Of Eden*, J. L. [Jack Warner] said that he'd heard Jimmy was still living on the lot. He was always against people staying on the lot because we had no insurance to cover

that, and there'd been a fire not long ago after some party that caused a lot of damage. He'd made an exception in Jimmy's case because Gadge [Kazan] had asked him, but after *Eden* he wanted Jimmy off the lot.

'I was talking to Jimmy every day because he'd asked me how he could get a weekly salary and I told him by signing a long-term contract – which meant we could use him for more pictures, but then the salary would be the same through the year instead of per picture. J. L. called and told me to have Jimmy off the lot by the end of the week. On Friday I asked the guard at the gate to let Jimmy in until Monday, that he still didn't have a place to live and was working at finding one, and he'd definitely have a place by the weekend.

77

'When Jimmy came back on the lot on Monday, all his luggage and clothes were waiting at the gate for him. He asked permission to go into the dressing room, and he reached into a vase and pulled out a couple of thousand dollars he'd been hiding – I think it was about $3,500.

'From that day on Jimmy never spoke to me voluntarily. He never came into my office again.' – Bill Orr, Warner Brothers executive

Jimmy's resentment of this high-handed treatment by Warners put his already strained relationship with them onto an even more hostile footing.
'Screw Hollywood, screw Jack Warner. Fuck the system. Shit on the producers, the guys in the middle, the moneymen in the East. Shit on the stars, the cult of personality, the phoney glamour. The best thing that can

happen out here is for a fuckin' great earthquake like the one they had in San Francisco to shake the whole lathe-and-plaster idiocy down to powdered rubble.

'Then maybe some of us who survived could go out in the streets with lightweight cameras and shoot the naked reality of existence. Imagine the rats and gophers and wild dogs running around the ruins feeding on the bodies of all the fat studio bums who died of fright after the few tremors of the 'quake.

'That's what these bastards are doing all the time, eating each other, acting out ritual murders and tortures, and cursing their enemies and banishing the faces that don't fit into the wilderness. When these guys have some goon threaten you, saying you'll wake up in the desert outside Vegas buried up to

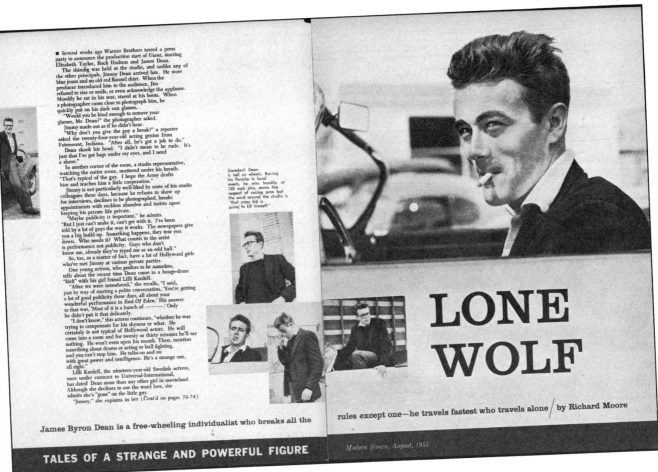

■ Several weeks ago Warner Brothers tossed a press party to announce the production start of *Giant*, starring Elizabeth Taylor, Rock Hudson and James Dean.

The shindig was held at the studio, and unlike any of the other principals, Jimmy Dean arrived late. He wore blue jeans and an old red flannel shirt. When the producer introduced him to the audience, Jim refused to rise or smile, or even acknowledge the applause. Moodily he sat in his seat, stared at his boots. When a photographer came close to photograph him, he quickly put on his dark sun glasses.

"Would you be kind enough to remove your glasses, Mr. Dean?" the photographer asked.

Jimmy made out as if he didn't hear.

"Why don't you give the guy a break?" a reporter asked the twenty-four-year-old acting genius from Fairmount, Indiana. "After all, he's got a job to do."

Dean shook his head. "I didn't mean to be rude. It's just that I've got bags under my eyes, and I need a shave."

In another corner of the room, a studio representative, watching the entire scene, muttered under his breath. "That's typical of the guy. I hope the Army drafts him and teaches him a little cooperation."

Jimmy is not particularly well-liked by some of his studio colleagues these days, because he refuses to show up for interviews, declines to be photographed, breaks appointments with reckless abandon and insists upon keeping his private life private.

"Maybe publicity *is* important," he admits. "But I just can't make it, can't get with it. I've been told by a lot of guys the way it works. The newspapers give you a big build-up. Something happens, they tear you down. Who needs it? What counts to the artist is performance not publicity. Guys who don't know me, already they've typed me as an odd ball."

So, too, as a matter of fact, have a lot of Hollywood girls who've met Jimmy at various private parties.

One young actress, who prefers to be nameless, tells about the recent time Dean came to a bongo-drum "kick" with his girl friend Lilli Kardell.

"After we were introduced," she recalls, "I said, just by way of starting a polite conversation, 'You're getting a lot of good publicity these days, all about your wonderful performance in *East Of Eden*.' His answer to that was, 'Most of it is a bunch of ———.' Only he didn't put it that delicately.

"I don't know," this actress continues, "whether he was trying to compensate for his shyness or what. He certainly is not typical of Hollywood actors. He will come into a room and for twenty or thirty minutes he'll say nothing. He won't even open his mouth. Then, mention something about drums or acting or bull fighting, and you can't stop him. He talks on and on with great power and intelligence. He's a strange one, all right."

Lilli Kardell, the nineteen-year-old Swedish actress, once under contract to Universal-International, has dated Dean more than any other girl in movieland. Although she declines to use the word love, she admits she's "gone" on the little guy.

"Jimmy," she explains in her (Cont'd on pages 70-74)

Daredevil Dean is hell on wheels. Racing his Porsche in local meets, he wins handily at 120 mph plus, earns the respect of racing pros but the word around the studio is "that crazy kid is going to kill himself."

LONE WOLF

James Byron Dean is a free-wheeling individualist who breaks all the rules except one—he travels fastest who travels alone / by Richard Moore

TALES OF A STRANGE AND POWERFUL FIGURE

Modern Screen, August, 1955

Below: Even during his lifetime, the movie gossip-mongers loved to point up the unhappy aspects of Jimmy's life, such as his mother's death and his break-up with Pier Angeli.

Happier days when Pier Angeli was his girl. He met her on the Warner lot while he was making "East Of Eden."

Aptly, he's in "Rebel Without A Cause."

Only a lasting love can cure the heartache he now knows. Will he someday recapture the happiness which he had — and held too briefly?

By Hope Gardner

A YOUNG man of medium height walked quickly down a darkened Los Angeles Street. He spoke to no one, he wanted no one to speak to him. He was desperately unhappy, lonely—and bitter. Only that day the girl Jimmy Dean loved had become another man's wife.

For Jimmy Dean did love Pier Angeli with all his heart. He wanted her as a wife. She was the one he was sure could cure his loneliness and heartache. Happiness had never been a part of Jimmy's life.

When he was a mere baby his mother died and left him to be raised by an uncle and aunt on a farm near Fairmount, Indiana. They were good to him, but always he yearned for the love of a real mother, for a family of his own. So early in life he withdrew into himself. He started mistrusting people, particularly women. Though he certainly did not blame his aunt for her lack of warmth, he felt somehow that he had been let down. He vowed to give his life to himself alone, to be very careful whom he trusted.

He set his aim—he wanted to be an actor. After high school he enrolled at the University of California at Los Angeles where he studied law and participated in college dramatics. Two years of this and he decided to go after an acting career realistically. He had a few hundred dollars which he took with him to New York and a little hotel off Times Square. And he started looking for an acting job in earnest. Though he got a few bit parts, nobody was overpowered by him—until he landed a job as a sailor aboard a sloop whose owner had theatrical connections.

It didn't matter to him that he knew nothing about sailing. He knew he'd learn. It worked and the skipper arranged for an interview for him which ended in his getting a highly dramatic role in "See the Jaguar." Other good roles followed, including the black-mailing Arab of "The Immoralist." TV too offered him strong dramatic roles. Jimmy Dean was launched. It was only natural that Hollywood would call him.

Jimmy Dean had no preconceived notion of Hollywood as was the case of Marlo Brando whose parting remark, when he left Manhattan for the film capitol, was: "I have not enough moral fortitude to turn down so much money." Jimmy was silent. He wanted to appear in pictures. He would take Hollywood as it came—when he got there. Hollywood baffled him. Making pictures did not. He resented the probing into his personal affairs. He hated what he called the insincerity of so many people. He said little, but he frowned a lot. Meantime he was starred in "East Of Eden", then in "Giant."

He dated girls and grew ill when they talked of nothing but "a break." He felt he was being used to help further their careers.

And then—when he was at his most indifferent about girls, he met Pier Angeli. It was obvious to him from the beginning that this girl, a top star, wanted nothing from him but his friendship. He started to dream—to hope that she would also want his love. And she did—for a while, until her mother stepped in and started *(Continued on page 71)*

"Rebel" director Nick Ray and Jimmy, who is in "Giant", also.

Another young star — Natalie Wood is his co-star and friend.

JAMES DEAN'S SECRET HEARTBREAK

the neck with an orange stuck in your mouth, they ain't kidding. They're killers, man, killers. We should put up with such shit? When Los Angeles returns to the desert and the Navajos take back their land, that will be the time to make the big Hollywood epic. *Gone With The Wind* will look like a home movie beside my picture: when the shit hit the fan.' – *Jimmy Dean*

But the shit hit the fan in an unexpected way for Jimmy when, having returned from a quick trip to New York, he was devastated to find that Pier Angeli had announced her engagement to the singer Vic Damone. She had met him the day Jimmy left for New York and by the next morning Damone had asked the Pierangelis for their daughter's hand in marriage. As Damone was a respectable Italian boy, Pier's parents were relieved

and delighted with the match and arranged for the ceremony to be held only a fortnight later on 24 November 1954. Jimmy's reaction to the news was one of horror.

'Oh no, please say you're kidding me!'
– *Jimmy Dean*

'When Jimmy learned that Pier had rejected him in favour of Vic Damone, the popular singer, he was thrown into a state of depression. Although he had tried to keep his true feelings well guarded, a closely personal matter, he had been unable to keep them from himself. He was too human to avoid the hurt that came from rejection. All he knew was that the relief of love had been denied him once again, leaving him with the ever-present, seldom-quieted compulsion to fulfil the undefined obligation that haunted him.

79

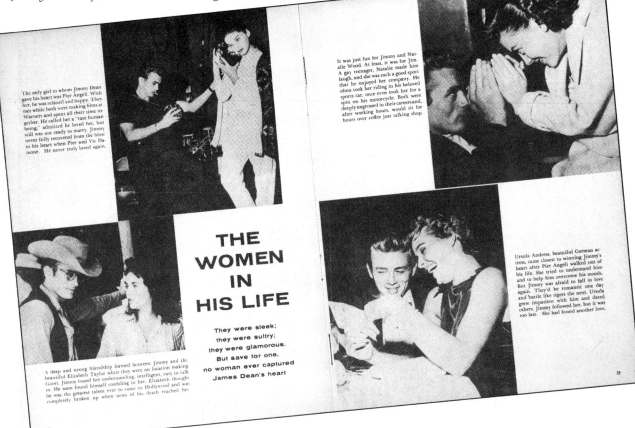

The only girl to whom Jimmy Dean gave his heart was Pier Angeli. With her, he was relaxed and happy. They met while both were making films at Warners and spent all their time together. He called her a "rare human being," admitted he loved her, but still was not ready to marry. Jimmy never fully recovered from the blow to his heart when Pier wed Vic Damone. He never truly loved again.

It was just fun for Jimmy and Natalie Wood. At least, it was for Jimmy. A gay teenager, Natalie made him laugh, and she was such a good sport that he enjoyed her company. He often took her riding in his beloved sports car, once even took her for a spin on his motorcycle. Both were deeply engrossed in their careers and, after working hours, would sit for hours over coffee just talking shop.

THE WOMEN IN HIS LIFE

They were sleek;
they were sultry;
they were glamorous.
But save for one,
no woman ever captured
James Dean's heart

A deep and strong friendship formed between Jimmy and the beautiful Elizabeth Taylor when they were on location making *Giant*. Jimmy found her understanding, intelligent, easy to talk to. He soon found himself confiding in her. Elizabeth thought he was the greatest talent ever to come to Hollywood and was completely broken up when news of his death reached her.

Ursula Andress, beautiful German actress, came closest to winning Jimmy's heart after Pier Angeli walked out of his life. She tried to understand him and to help him overcome his moods. But Jimmy was afraid to fall in love again. They'd be romantic one day and battle like tigers the next. Ursula grew impatient with him and dated others. Jimmy followed her, but it was too late. She had found another love.

'Around Hollywood, rumour had it that, on the day Pier married Vic, Jimmy sat on his motorcycle across from the church and cried. In any case he was deeply hurt and terribly disappointed. In his persistent effort to partake of all emotions to the fullest, when he loved, he allowed himself to love completely, and when he lost the object of his love, he allowed himself to suffer completely.' – *Bill Bast*

'You might say I'm not exactly delighted and happy over her marriage to Vic. I've seen Pat Hardy a few times and I'd say she was a little hurt too. I guess she and Vic were practically engaged. He'd call her parents and everything. She was surprised when Vic and Pier announced their engagement. But something happened. I figure that when I got back to New York after finishing *East Of Eden* her family and friends got her ear and changed her mind about me.

'I won't try to pretend I'm not sorry

– Pier's still OK with me. She broke the news to me the night before she announced her engagement, but she wouldn't tell me who the guy was. I was floored when I learned it was Vic Damone. Oh well, maybe she likes his singing. I hope they'll be happy.' – *Jimmy Dean*

But the couple weren't happy. Only five years later Pier divorced Damone and then entered into another unhappy marriage with the musician Armando Trotajoli. She was haunted by the memories of her happy times with Jimmy.
'He is the only man I ever loved deeply as a woman should love a man. I never loved either of my husbands the way I loved Jimmy.

'I tried to love my husbands but it never lasted. I would wake up in the night and find I had been dreaming of Jimmy. I would lie awake in the same bed with my husband, think of my love for Jimmy and wish it was Jimmy and not my husband who was next to me.

Below: Jimmy backstage in New York with the actress Geraldine Page, one of many friends on whom he would drop in unannounced. Bottom: Jimmy was a notorious insomniac who would catnap whenever he could.

'I had to separate from my husbands because I don't think one can be in love with one man – even if he is dead – and live with another.' – *Pier Angeli*

Jimmy's solution to his heartbreak was to drown his sorrows by drinking, and his drunken violent behaviour alienated some of his friends, among them Leonard Rosenman, who was writing the musical score for East Of Eden.
'He was in a period of life where he drank a good deal. And he was just drunk and disorderly. And I guess I had just outgrown that kind of thing.' – *Leonard Rosenman*

Rosenman also suggested that Jimmy's drinking had contributed to the break-up with Pier in the

Jimmy's death made a profound impact on European as well as American cinemagoers. His reputation as an anti-hero particularly appealed to French readers of 'Cinémonde' (below).

Cinémonde ainsi parlait celui qui fut **JAMES DEAN**

Si un homme peut franchir le gouffre qui sépare la vie de la mort, s'il se survit, alors, peut-être, a-t-il accompli quelque chose.

Bien sûr... Mais tu veux être acteur... Pour être acteur, il faut tout connaître, tout éprouver, tout essayer... Ne serait-ce qu'une fois, une seule et unique fois...

En vérité, il n'y a rien à quoi l'on ne puisse prétendre, à condition d'y mettre le prix. Les gens ont peur de trop réussir et je sais pourquoi. C'est que la réussite est une responsabilité terrible...

Toi aussi, tu trouves cela idiot. Mais avoir peur et aller jusqu'au bout de sa peur, tu ne trouves pas cela formidablement excitant ? Se dire qu'on peut mourir...

'EAST of EDEN'

Cast of Characters:

Abra..............Julie Harris   Kate..............Jo Van Fleet
Cal..............James Dean   Sheriff Cooper......Burl Ives
Adam..........Raymond Massey   Mr. Hamilton..Albert Dekker
Aron..........Richard Davalos   Ann..............Lois Smith

When Broadway director Elia Kazan was called to the coast to convert John Steinbeck's mammoth novel of good and evil to the screen, he insisted on picking his own cast. First, he signed Julie Harris and Raymond Massey for major roles. Then for the key roles of the twin brothers, he tapped two young unknowns, James Dean and Richard Davalos. Dean was fresh from Broadway, where he had parlayed a small, but telling, part in *The Immoralist* into award-winning proportions. Jo Van Fleet, Burl Ives and Lois Smith completed the off-beat (by Hollywood standards) cast.

With this group, he set about making this explosive movie, a modernized version of the Cain and Abel biblical legend. It's the passionate story of twin brothers, one good, the other bad, and a father who parcels out his love on a merit basis.

What resulted was a moving and powerful drama. But what has lasted are the performances of his stars. Here, in pictures is the story which catapulted James Dean to stardom.

1. Young Cal Trask follows notorious woman named Kate in neighboring town, Monterey, finds she runs a gambling hall.

2. After being chased away by her henchman, Cal broods over Kate on the way home to Salinas. He thinks she's his mother.

3. Twin brother Aron chides Cal for staying out all night as he takes his girl, Abra, to see icehouse their father bought.

4. Adam Trask tells friend Will Hamilton of far-sighted plan he has for shipping lettuce east in freight cars packed with ice.

5. Exploring icehouse, Aron and Abra hide from Cal and discuss his strange actions and his inability to please father, Adam.

6. The lonely, misunderstood boy overhears their conversation and vents his frustration by hurling ice down the chute.

7. That evening, Adam compares the sullen Cal to his brother and punishes the hurt boy by making him read the B...

8. Cal sneaks out again and goes to Kate's Salinas gambling ... A frightened barmaid, Ann, shows him Kate's chambers.

9. Cal sneaks into Kate's room, finds her sleeping in a chair, and sits silently watching her until she awakes with a start.

10. The angry woman has helper throw the boy out. Cal desperately tries to ask if she's his mother, but Kate won't listen.

first place.
'Jimmy would get drunk on a couple of glasses of wine, and when he got drunk he could become very nasty. His personality completely changed; he was completely uncontrollable and could get vicious. It was very Jekyll and Hyde. He also became violent, and he had a reputation for beating up his girlfriends. He did this to Pier once too often and I think she just had enough.' – *Leonard Rosenman*

But then Jimmy's mind was distracted by the build-up to the release of East Of Eden, *which everyone suspected was going to be a big event.*
'At the very end of shooting, the last few days, you felt that a star was going to be born. Everybody smelled it; all the publicity people began to hang around him.' – *Elia Kazan*

Jimmy made a few concessions to the press, and agreed to Frank Worth taking some publicity shots. But he was still very conscious of how his image came across. He stressed to Worth that one particular photo taken at the session should not be published. When asked why he answered:
'It makes me look like a kid. A helpless kid who just got his finger banged or his best toy busted and he wants his mother. It makes me look like I'm hurt and crying out – not out loud – but just crying for someone to come and help me. I don't want people to see me that way.' – *Jimmy Dean*

Jimmy also gave a rare interview to The New York Times. *In the interview he was asked whether he really belonged to the stage or to the screen.*
'As of now, I don't consider myself as specifically belonging to either. The cinema is a very truthful medium because the camera doesn't let you get away with anything. On stage, you can even loaf a little, if you're so inclined. Technique, on the other hand, is more important. My real aim, my real goal, is to achieve what I call camera functioning on stage.'– *Jimmy Dean*

But he never got the chance to act on stage again. Once the preview of East Of Eden *was shown, Jimmy Dean was already immortalised as a Hollywood icon. Jimmy went to the preview with Bill Bast, and was clearly apprehensive about what everyone would think. His sheepish way of inviting Bast to the showing indicated how nervous he was about it.*
'Ah Willie, *Eden* is previewing tonight, if you want to see it.' – *Jimmy Dean*

But there was an electric atmosphere in the theatre that night and Jimmy sensed that his performance had gone down well.
'Pretty good, wasn't I?' – *Jimmy Dean*

The critics' reviews of the film were on the whole ecstatic. Even Hedda Hopper changed her mind about this 'dirty shirt-tail actor'.
'In the projection room I sat spellbound. I couldn't remember ever having seen a young man with such power, so many facets of expression, so much sheer invention as this actor.' – *Hedda Hopper*

But The New York Times *critic Bosley Crowther was deeply scathing about Jimmy's performance and passed him off as another Brando clone.*
'The people in *East Of Eden* are not sufficiently well established to give point to the anguish through which they go. Especially this is true of James Dean in the role of the confused and cranky Cal. This young actor, who is here doing his first big screen stint, is a mass of histrionic gingerbread.
'He scuffs his feet, he whirls, he pouts, he sputters, he leans against walls, he rolls his eyes, he swallows his words, he ambles slack-kneed – all like Marlon Brando used to do. Never have we seen a performer so clearly follow another's style. Mr Kazan should be spanked for permitting him to do such a sophomoric thing. Whatever there might be of reasonable torment in this youngster is buried beneath clumsy display.' – *Bosley Crowther*

'The best way to describe Jimmy Dean quickly, is to say he is Marlon Brando seven years ago.' – *Sidney Skolsky, columnist*

Although Brando had been his earlier idol, Jimmy was far from flattered by the constant comparisons between the two actors.
'People were telling me I behaved like Brando before I knew who Brando was. I am not disturbed by the comparison, nor am I flattered. I have my own personal rebellions and I don't have to rely on Brando's. However, it's true I am constantly reminding people of him. People discover resemblances: we are both from farms, dress as we please, ride motorcycles and work for Elia Kazan. As an actor I have no desire to behave like Brando – and I don't attempt to. Nevertheless, it is very difficult not to be impressed, not to carry the image of a highly successful actor. But that's as far as it goes. I feel within myself there are expressions just as valid and I'll have a few years to develop my own style.' – *Jimmy Dean*

Jimmy was rather taken aback by the furore his film seemed to be creating. He was supposed to attend the glitzy gala première of the film in New York, but just couldn't take the exposure. He made his excuses to his agent Jane Deacy.
'I'm sorry, Mom, but you know I can't make this scene. I can't handle it. So I'm going back to the Coast tonight.' – *Jimmy Dean*

Warners were furious that their main star of the evening didn't turn up, but already Jimmy was becoming one of the most talked-about actors of the year. And Jimmy's road to screen stardom, already paved with Eden *gold, took another bold step forward when he agreed to work with Nick Ray on* Rebel Without A Cause. *His gruff acceptance of the role revealed an increasing mistrust of Warners.*
'I want to do your film, but don't let them bastards [Warners] hear about it.' – *Jimmy Dean to Nick Ray*

Chapter 5

REBEL WITHOUT A CAUSE

'The drama of his life was the drama of desiring to belong…The intensity of his desires, his fears, could make the search at times arrogant, egocentric; but behind it was such a desperate vulnerability that one was moved, even frightened.'
Nick Ray

Perhaps more than any other, the role of Jim Stark in Rebel Without a Cause *casts Jimmy as the ultimate teenage hero, an image as powerful today as it was in the fifties. The film revolves around Jim's first day at Dawson High School and how he copes with being a new kid in a new town. Already estranged from his domineering mother and henpecked father, Jim is soon on the wrong side of the law and of the local bad-boy gang which is led by Buzz (Corey Allen). Challenged to a teenage duel by Buzz, Jim finds himself in yet more trouble when the chicken-run they have set up goes disastrously wrong and Buzz is killed. Jim makes off to a deserted mansion with his new girlfriend Judy (Natalie Wood) and ends the film a hero when he tries to protect the school wimp, Plato (Sal Mineo), from the trigger-happy local police force. Like Elia Kazan before him, Nick Ray realised that much of Jimmy's own personality was inherent in the role he was to play in the film.*

'The drama of his life, I thought, after seeing him in New York, was the drama of desiring to belong…(so was Jim Stark's). It was a conflict of violent eagerness and mistrust created very young…The intensity of his desires, his fears, could make the search at times arrogant, egocentric; but behind it was such a desperate vulnerability that one was moved, even frightened.' – *Nick Ray*

Nick Ray was considered to be an unconventional film maker at the time – a rebel in his own right. Perhaps this is why he managed to forge a tremendously successful partnership with Jimmy – a partnership in which each man understood and admired the other.

'Since beginning to know him a little, I had realised that for a successful collaboration he needed a special kind of climate. He needed reassurance, tolerance, understanding. An important way of creating this climate was to involve him at every stage in the development of the picture.' – *Nick Ray*

'That man's a great human being, not like some of the bastards I've met in this town.' – *Jimmy Dean*

'The thing that interested me in *Rebel* was doing something that would counteract *The Wild One*. I went out and hung around with kids in Los Angeles before making the movie. Some of them even call themselves ''wild ones''. They wear leather jackets, go out looking for someone to rough up a little. These aren't poor kids, you know. Lots of them have money, grow up and become pillars of the community! Boy, they scared me! But it's a constructive movie, it gives some of these kids, the ones who aren't out to be tough guys, something to identify with.' – *Jimmy Dean*

Jimmy had some time to kill before shooting began on the film in March 1955. First, he went

The events of 'Rebel Without A Cause' take place within a 24 hour period, yet it takes in every facet of American high school life – from the flick knife fight (below) to the automobile culture (bottom).

back to Indiana to see his family and was accompanied by photographer Dennis Stock, who captured Jimmy in his native surroundings. With his distrust of all publicity stunts, Jimmy was not always pleasant to be around.

'He was a bastard sometimes, but I liked him well enough so that when he got into one of those moods, I would just pull away and not go near him for a while.' – Dennis Stock

But Dennis Stock was also given a rare insight into Jimmy's farmboy background, and the early forces which had moulded him. It soon became clear that one of Jimmy's most important memories of childhood was his mother's death. One day he pointed out Fairmount's undertakers.

'That's the firm that arranged my mother's funeral.' – Jimmy Dean

Left: 'Wish You Were Here, Jimmy Dean' (published in the 1980s), identified Dean's 'Rebel' image as the most enduring. Below: This macabre funeral parlour pose was Dean's own idea.

It was during these photo sessions that some of the most enduring and powerful images of Jimmy were captured, among them the famous shots of Jimmy posing inside a coffin, an idea which shocked the photographer.
'He wasn't being delightful about death. C'mon! *You* lay down in a coffin sometime and tell me what it's about. It's one thing not to be afraid of death and to be realistic about it, but he was afraid, *afraid*. And his way of dealing with it was to laugh in the demon's face, to make fun of it, tempt it, taunt it. He wasn't being cool about death at all. When Jimmy acted like this I just wanted to take him by the shoulders and shake him and say, ''How dare you!'' ' – *Dennis Stock*

But Jimmy did *dare. His chillingly morbid assessment of what it was like in a coffin showed an unhealthy obsession with death.*
'The creepiest thing about it was that with the lid shut, it squashes your nose.' – *Jimmy Dean*

'Man is cast into an unsympathetic world in which he tries to achieve purposes all of which will inevitably come to nought in death. He may come to evade the thought of his own coming dissolution by living his life in terms of impersonal and conventional generalities, but he can be true to himself only by living constantly with the thought of his own eventual death...Man is inevitably given over to care and subject to a fate to which he can close his eyes, but which he cannot escape.' – *Jimmy Dean*

Ironically, Jimmy would not live to see Fairmount again after this trip. He travelled back to Los Angeles to prepare for his new film role and almost at once began to develop his fatal passion for speed. He bought a Porsche sports car and decided to enter some local race meetings.
'Jimmy wanted speed. He wanted his body to hurtle across over the ground, the faster the

better. Jimmy was a straightaway driver. His track was the shortest distance between here and there.' – *Ken Miles, racing driver*

But he also got a kick out of dicing with death.
'I can flirt with death and come through.'
– *Jimmy Dean*

This belief in his charmed life was partly centred on a blind trust in the reliability of his new car.
'The thing about this car is that it's fail-safe...These brand new Porsches are made like tanks. They have the best engine and the best transmission, they're totally safe.'
– *Jimmy Dean*

Perhaps yet another reason for Jimmy's love of speed was an erotic fascination – it provided a spine-tingling alternative to sex.
'My sex pours itself into fast curves, broad-slides and broodings, drags etc...I have been

sleeping with my MG.' – *Jimmy Dean*

Jimmy entered five race meetings in all and managed to notch up six outright victories which fascinated the press, but didn't impress Warners. At first the film studio sat on the fence about his dangerous pastime.
'They sort of shoot around it, but they've never said, ''Don't do it.'' Everybody likes a winner, and so far I've been winning.' – *Jimmy Dean*

But eventually Warners took a tougher stand. After all, they had a lot of money invested in him and couldn't risk an accident slowing up the progress of the film. By this time Jimmy's antics were legendary.
'Jimmy was a dreadful driver. He would hit a hay bale every time he went around a corner. That's no way to drive, slamming your car around like a billiard ball. The pit crew who worked in the gas station across from Warners thought he was a bad driver too. One day I was in the gas station and

Jimmy came off the freeway on his motorcycle and down this steep grade that goes onto Barham Boulevard. His brakes failed, and his way of stopping was to cut across the street, run through the gas station and drive into a wall. That he didn't kill himself or crush a leg was a miracle.' – *Irving Shulman, who adapted* Rebel Without A Cause *from the book by Robert Lindner*

It was a sorry blow for Jimmy, who had found a reason to live again after the heartbreak over Pier Angeli.
'Racing is the only time I feel whole.' – *Jimmy Dean*

Predictably, Jimmy was angry with Warners for their dictatorial attitude.
' ''One crowded hour of glorious life is worth an age without a name.'' – Alan Seeger, poet.
   'That's the line I want put on my tombstone, can't you see it? That's what I want it to say...Tell Jack Warner.' – *Jimmy Dean*

Just as the racing storm died down, Warners had another problem with Jimmy when he disappeared only a couple of days before shooting on Rebel *began. Stewart Stern, who wrote the script for the film, was the first to discover what he had been up to.*
'A few days before shooting began, Jimmy disappeared. No one knew where he was and Warners was frantic, threatening to suspend him. Then one morning at about four o'clock my phone rings and I hear this ''Mmmmooooo.'' I knew it was Jimmy and I mooed back. Then I said, ''How are you?'' And Jimmy said he wasn't going to come back. He asked me if I thought he should do the movie, and I told him, ''If you did it and were miserable in it or if the picture turned out badly, then it would be on my head, and I couldn't take that responsibility.'' I told him they were thinking of suspending him.
   'Jimmy just said, ''Well, I'm not coming back. Talk to ya.''
   'He was gone about ten days, and then

Right: Dean's role in 'Rebel Without A Cause' helped title hundreds of appreciations. Below: Dean as Jim Stark in a pose which every misunderstood adolescent can identify with.

one day he just showed up at my office and looked at this perfectly blank wall, stood back pretending to admire an imaginary painting. I think he was looking at Picasso's *Guernica*. He asked me if it was real or a reproduction, and I said, ''Oh God, it's real of course!'' And he said, ''Well, you writers...and just because you're a nephew of Arthur Lowe...'' But he never talked about where he'd been or why he'd come back.

'I don't know what scared him, but I know he was scared.' – *Stewart Stern*

Jimmy was afraid of not being accepted as himself by the other members of the film's team.
'He was trying to get out of the role he felt he was being shoved into, whether as a son

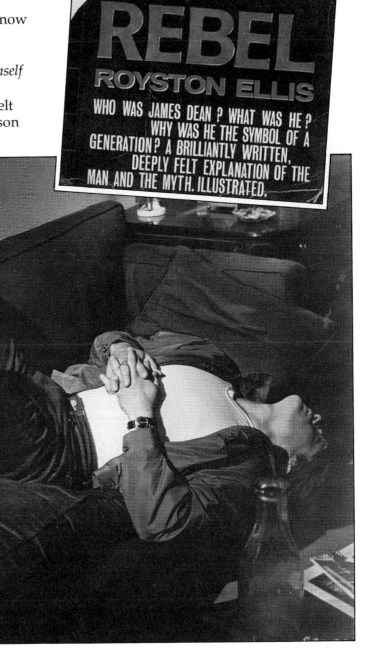

REBEL
ROYSTON ELLIS

3/6

WHO WAS JAMES DEAN? WHAT WAS HE? WHY WAS HE THE SYMBOL OF A GENERATION? A BRILLIANTLY WRITTEN, DEEPLY FELT EXPLANATION OF THE MAN AND THE MYTH. ILLUSTRATED.

or bad boy. Whatever it was, he wanted to be himself.' – *Stewart Stern*

A close friend of his at the time, John Gilmore, often used to listen to Jimmy's fears before he arrived at the Rebel *studio.*
'I don't know what it is but I'd rather be staying asleep, do you ever have the feeling that you're really scared the day isn't going to turn out the way you want it to, to be right?' – *Jimmy Dean*

'I'm going to call today off. I'm going back now.' – *Jimmy Dean*

But Jimmy's fears were to a large degree unfounded. He earned the respect and friendship of many of his co-actors.
'I never worked again with an actor like Jimmy. He didn't act a part, he lived it. He also went out of his way to help me, if I blew a scene he'd say, ''Don't worry, take it easy – you'll get it this time.'' He just never acted like a big star.' – *Sal Mineo*

Natalie Wood, who played the leading female role in the film and made her screen kiss début with Jimmy, became a close personal friend.
'I thought he was totally weird – until I began working with him.' – *Natalie Wood*

'He was so inspiring, always so patient and kind. He didn't act as though he were a star at all. We all gave each other suggestions, and he was very critical of himself, never satisfied with his work, and worried about how every scene would turn out. He was so great when he played a scene, he had the ability to make everyone else look great too. He used to come on the set and watch the scenes even when he wasn't in them. He was interested in the whole picture and not just in his own part.' – *Natalie Wood*

But, because Jimmy was such a perfectionist about the film, he would often make demands of himself which were not entirely popular with

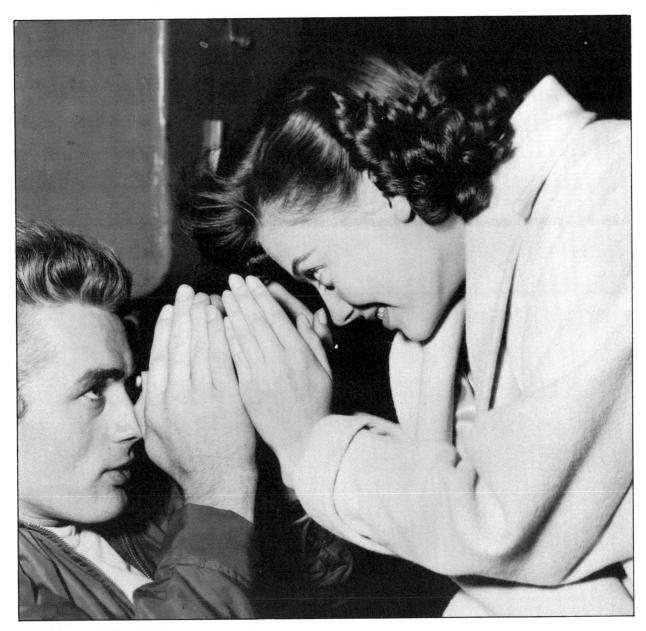

others involved. Sometimes he would hold up the whole proceedings when he was trying to get into the part. Jim Backus, who played Jim Stark's father, remembered how Jimmy got ready for the scene in which the hero frustratedly bangs his fist hard down on the desk of a police officer in the Juvenile Hall.

'He was preparing. He was drinking wine, hitting a drum and they were trying to get him on the set, but he wouldn't come out until he was ready. He kept them waiting several hours. Now, if you keep a set waiting, the executives up in the big building hear about it and descend in a covey of limousines.

'Anyhow, Jimmy walked out finally and said, "I'm ready", and he did that whole scene in one take. Beat the desk, broke two bones in his hand and as he walked off the set, the camera crew cheered. And you know what a hard-nosed bunch they are.' – *Jim Backus*

'Most actors wear a mask in order not to reveal themselves. This is easy. It is easy to show what a character is going through, but hard to do it.' – *Jimmy Dean*

'James Dean was the first guerilla artist ever to work in movies.' – *Dennis Hopper, co-actor in* Rebel

'He throws everything into his acting, and I

have bruises on my arm to prove it.' – *Natalie Wood*

Jimmy really seemed to be finding himself as an actor and was actually realising his own personal credo.
'When you know there's something more to go in the character, and you're not sure what it is, you just got to go out after it. Walk out on the tight-rope. If the rope's hard it's got to be leading somewhere.' – *Jimmy Dean*

'To be a fine actor you must remember two things – concentration and unlimited imagination. With those, there's no limit to what you can do. Develop them, and you'll develop.'– *Jimmy Dean*

'All of us were touched by Jimmy and he was touched by greatness.' – *Natalie Wood*

But Jimmy was lucky that his potential was being given free rein by the director, Nick Ray, who allowed him to impose his own interpretation on

the film.
'James Dean worked very closely with Nick. May I say that this is the first time in the history of motion pictures that a twenty-four-year-old boy, with only one movie to his credit, was practically the co-director. Jimmy insisted on utter realism, and, looking back, I sometimes wonder how we finished so violent a picture without someone getting seriously injured.' – *Jim Backus*

When, during a knife fight scene, Nick Ray tried to cut the action because a thin trickle of blood was running down Jimmy's neck, he wished he hadn't.
'What the hell are you doing?' Can't you see I'm having a real moment? Don't you ever cut a scene while I'm having a real moment. What the fuck do you think I'm here for?' – *Jimmy Dean*

Jimmy later defended the raw, real violence of the scene in a newspaper interview.
'In motion pictures you can't fool with the

Below: Rarely has one film star so exactly matched the roles he played. Right: The scene in 'Rebel' in which things finally boil over between the misunderstood son and his repressed suburban parents.

camera. If we were doing this on stage, we'd probably be able to gimmick it up – but not in a picture. Film fans are too critical these days.' – *Jimmy Dean*

Jimmy was also very determined that he should do the 'chicken-run' scene himself and not allow a stuntman to stand in for him. The chicken-run is the most dramatic episode in the film where Jim Stark and Buzz in their stolen cars hurtle towards a cliff, the idea being that the first one to jump clear is a coward or 'chicken'. In a typical instance of life imitating art, Jimmy was adamant that no one should think him chicken for not daring to do a dangerous stunt. He therefore refused to have a mattress waiting for him at the end of the set to soften his landing.

'Take it away, Limey. People will say, ''James Dean can't even do his own stunts, he needs

a mattress.'' ' – *Jimmy Dean*

Apart from these differences of opinion, Jimmy and Nick succeeded in forming a creative and harmonious team based on mutual respect and understanding.

'A director should be an intelligent and competent guide for the actor. When an actor plays a scene exactly the way a director orders, it isn't acting. It's following instruction. Anyone with the physical qualifications can do that. So the director's task is just that, to direct, to point the way. Then the actor must take over. And he must be allowed the space, the freedom, to express himself in the role. Without that space an actor is no more than an unthinking robot with a chestful of push-buttons.' – *Jimmy Dean*

'At the time I worked with him, I thought he would surpass…without a doubt, would surpass Brando, Mithure, Gérard Philipe, Olivier. And I revise my opinion only in terms of Larry.' – *Nick Ray*

But although things seemed to be going well for Jimmy professionally, he still avoided close personal relationships and became something of a loner on the Rebel *set.*

'He was the child who goes to a secret corner and refuses to speak.' – *Nick Ray*

'He was very protective of himself. He was a sensitive guy and my feeling is that he didn't really allow people into him because he was busy protecting this awareness that he had, and he didn't want to be split off socially and find himself playing games, so he stayed to himself. When he felt very secure then occasionally he would open up.' – *Corey Allen*

'Sometimes Jimmy wouldn't even hear you when you spoke to him, he would just switch off, he could concentrate totally, but he was always polite and nice to be with. At that time a lot of big people were snubbing him, maybe they were frightened of this startling new talent that was so completely different from anything we knew at the time. If those people think their pools or their Cadillacs are threatened, they pull up the drawbridge quickly.'– *Natalie Wood*

Fairly predictably, Jimmy seemed to be antagonising anyone who was 'big', especially those involved in the image-building of Hollywood. Jimmy was becoming increasingly sceptical of the publicity hyenas he was meant to humour. When told he was receiving a lot of publicity he replied with typical hostility:

'Most of it is a bunch of shit.' – *Jimmy Dean*

*'The James Dean Anniversary Book' was one of many
to dissect the film's treatment of teenage issues, daring
to show the realities of the school yard in a serious,
dramatic way.*

When Jimmy found that Warners had put his
picture up on the wall in their offices, he made a
big fuss.
'Don't you ever put my fucking picture up
here! Whatta you think, that I live here or
something? You think you own me? Nobody
owns me!' – *Jimmy Dean*

He was equally hostile on the set of Rebel, *when
a Warners executive wanted to know if Jimmy was
going to do a Mr Magoo impression in the scene
where he is looking around a deserted mansion
with Judy and Plato.*
Studio executive: 'I understand you're doing
Mr Magoo in this scene?'
Jimmy Dean: 'What business is it of yours
what I'm doing?'
Studio executive: 'You know this is Warner
Brothers?'
Jimmy Dean: 'Yeah, I've got the general idea.'
Studio executive: 'Well, as long as this is

Warner Brothers, why don't you make it Bugs
Bunny?'
Jimmy Dean: 'Get your ass out of here!'

*Jimmy's excuse for antagonising such people was
that it was what they expected of their new 'rebel'
star.*
'Aw, they love it, they eat it up.' – *Jimmy
Dean*

*Many people in the media despised Jimmy, too.
One magazine editor who was being shown some
photographs for a story on him commented:*
'I like the pictures, but I can't stand the
subject.'

*One columnist whose favour Jimmy courted was
Hedda Hopper who had originally given him such
scathing reports. But she had been transfixed by
his performance in* East of Eden *and was now
eating out of his hand. Jimmy referred to her as:*

102

'My friend at Court.'

Surprisingly, Jimmy really made an effort to turn on the charm for Hedda. He defended such uncharacteristic behaviour thus:
'Look at it as protective coloration. If I conform to myself, the only one I'm hurting with the press is myself. So, instead, I'm a nice, polite, well-raised young boy full of respect – which is what Hedda likes. Instead of being on my back, she'll be on my side and she'll defend me against the other press, the people who say I'm an irresponsible, no-good rebel.' – *Jimmy Dean*

By May 1955 the shooting on Rebel *had finished. Jimmy and Nick, aware that they had created something very special, were sad to have to say goodbye to the film.*
'Jimmy and I were left alone on the lot at Warners; everyone but the gateman had gone home. We were wandering around under the lights making sure we hadn't left anything behind. We really didn't want to admit it was all over. I said, ''Let's go. We've nothing more to do here.''
'Dean climbed on his motorbike and I climbed in my car and we raced into town very fast. On Hollywood Boulevard he spread himself like a flying angel on the bike with his feet up on the back mudguard, his arms outstretched, and sped off with a roar. Then we stopped at a traffic light to say goodnight – and even then we couldn't really admit it was all over. So we found an all-night restaurant and had an early breakfast.' – *Nick Ray*

Jimmy looked back on the valuable things he had learnt while making the film, and on the friendships he had formed.
'Never has an acting job taken so much out

of me. I put everything I had into that one and I am pleased with the general result. Any writer, musician, painter or actor will tell you that when they look back on their work they know it could be improved, but in the end you have to say, ''OK, that's it. It's finished. It stands or falls as it is.'' I now regard Natalie, Nick and Sal not as co-workers, I regard them as friends, about the only friends I have in this town and I hope we all work together soon.'– *Jimmy Dean*

Jimmy especially wanted to work again with Nick Ray, who had helped him to develop and extend talents both as an actor and as a director. Jimmy told Ray about his hopes to further his career as a director and a writer.

'Acting is just interpretation, I want to create for myself.' – *Jimmy Dean*

'Acting is wonderful and immediately satisfying but my talents lie in directing and,

beyond that, my great fear is writing. That's the god. I can't apply the seat of my pants right now. I'm too youthful and silly. I must have some age. I'm in great awe of writing and fearful of it...but some day...' – *Jimmy Dean*

Nothing ever came of this dream to write, but we can be sure that if Jimmy had turned his talents in this direction, the results would have been unconventional. He had already expressed forcibly his feelings of contempt for establishment literature.

'The masterpieces are on the rack, I just put the goddamned fuckers up to dry.' – *Jimmy Dean*

When the first previews of Rebel *were released, many realised how successful the Dean/Ray partnership had been – Jimmy's portrayal of Jim*

Stark was disarmingly powerful. Sal Mineo was in the projection room with Jimmy when he first watched the film.

'He was sitting there just behind me, and half a dozen times when he was really terrific, I turned around to look at him. He was giving that grin of his and almost blushing, looking at the floor.' – *Sal Mineo*

'When you saw *Rebel Without A Cause*, that was Jimmy you were seeing up there on the screen.' – *Dennis Stock*

But Jimmy never saw the film released, never knew what a huge impact it had on teenagers around the world. With a grim irony, he survived the chicken-run car race on screen, but only four days before the film came out, Jimmy became the victim of speed in a fatal car crash near Paso Robles.

Chapter 6

GIANT

'You could feel the loneliness beating out
of him, and it hit you like a wave. You
can forgive a lot of things for talent and
Jimmy was bursting with it.'
Mercedes McCambridge

*Jimmy made one last film before his death,
which would stand as the final part in a legendary
trilogy. He had met the great Hollywood director
George Stevens around the Warners lot, and really
wanted to land the part of Jett Rink in Stevens'
next film* Giant.

*He had wormed his way into Stevens' circle by
courting favour with his cronies, among them
Fred Guoil who was Stevens' assistant.*
'When Jimmy was working with Gadge
[Elia Kazan], he would walk back and forth
past our office every day, and soon he started
to drop in to talk to Freddy Guoil. When
he first came into the office, my secretary was
a little concerned about him being there;
she didn't know him from Adam. Jimmy and
Fred talked about cars and fishing and stuff –
not very fast-moving conversation, mind you
– every five minutes or so somebody said a
word.
    'When *East Of Eden* was finished we went
to see it, and the boy was just incredible. I'm
not just talking about him as an actor, but
it was his acting that made his personality so
sensitive. So when we cast the role of Jett
Rink – which really called for a tough, kind
of beefy guy – I said to Fred, "Hold onto
your belt, Fred. What do you think of Jimmy
Dean for the part?" So the next day I said,
"Here Jim, I want you to take a look at this
script and see how you feel about it. See
if it's too far out for you." He said, "Okay".
There was about a half hour of conversation
between us. After no haste at all, he read
it, came back to my office, put the book on
the table and stood there and shook his head.
Now Jimmy Dean had a way of shaking his
head so that it could be both positive and
negative. He'd shake it up and down, but
you'd catch an angle of negative in it. I could
never imitate it. Anyway Jimmy shook his
head and said, "That'd be a good thing." We
talked some more and he decided to do it.'
– George Stevens*

Jimmy seemed very positive about the part he

GIANT

Cast of Characters:

Jett Rink	James Dean	Luz	Mercedes McCambridge
Leslie	Elizabeth Taylor	Uncle Bawley	Chill Wills
Bick	Rock Hudson	Luz II	Carroll Baker
Vashti	Jane Withers	Jordy	Dennis Hopper

From the very start, Edna Ferber's gigantic novel of Texas created a furor. It's rumored that some of that mighty state's citizens suggested she be burned in effigy on the capital lawn, for the story jabbed unmercifully at Texan aristocracy.
    Nor did the heat die down when casting was announced for the movie. Because the book chronicles the rise of a Texas millionaire over a 30-year period, the cast had to age progressively as the years went by.
    It's to their credit that they were able to carry a story of this scope. But even more responsible was producer-director *par excellence*, George Stevens, who coaxed such performances from his stars that even now *Giant* is being touted as next year's Oscar winner. No small part of that tribute will be James Dean's, for this was a once-in-a-lifetime role for any actor.
    Here, then, in pictures, is Jimmy's final and greatest performance.

1. Texas cattleman Bick Benedict goes to Virginia to buy horses, but meets aristocratic Leslie Lynnton instead, sweeps her off her feet.

4. Rebellious young ranch hand, Jett Rink, taunts Leslie about the callous attitude of her husband toward his Mexican workers.

7. As years go by, Leslie and Bick have three beautiful children. Proud Bick is sure they eventually will take over the huge ranch.

8. But their married life falls flat and Leslie constantly badgers Bick about improving the living conditions of their servants.

40

*would play – a surly cowboy who strikes oil and
becomes corrupted by the influence and power his
new wealth brings. He told Bill Bast:*
'I sure would like to get my teeth into the Jett
Rink part.' – Jimmy Dean

*He was in awe of the impressive cast list,
which included Rock Hudson and the Queen of
Hollywood, Elizabeth Taylor. But most of all
Jimmy had wanted to work with someone as
famous and established as George Stevens.*
'George Stevens, the greatest of them all...
this guy was born with the movies. So
real, unassuming. You'll be talking to him,
thinking he missed your point, and then,
bang! – he has it.' – Jimmy Dean

Many of the cast and crew of Giant *were
a little apprehensive about working with Jimmy,
whose uncooperative and rude behaviour was now*

'Giant' was Jimmy Dean's last role before his death – like 'Rebel Without A Cause', it was released posthumously.

After their marriage, Bick takes Leslie to Reata Ranch. She meets Vashti Snythe, a rich local belle who lost out with Bick.

3. Leslie is amazed at Bick's vast empire, also at the money-consciousness of the wealthy cattle millionaires she meets.

He shows her the squalor of their quarters, the poverty they must endure, while Bick's money is used only to expand the ranch.

6. Leslie tends neglected baby for helpless wife of Bick's chauffeur and embarks on life-long crusade to better their conditions.

9. Big argument sends Leslie and the children back to Virginia. Bick is broken-hearted, but remains adamant in his iron rule.

10. Refined life of Virginia still appeals to Leslie, but she misses Bick, is overjoyed when he finally comes back to reclaim her.

41

Bick Benedict était venu au Maryland pour acheter un magnifique étalon noir pour son vaste domaine de Reata, au Texas. Mais au haras, il avait rencontré la fille des éleveurs, la ravissante Leslie, si différente de toutes les femmes qu'il avait jusqu'alors connues. Il en devint aussitôt amoureux.

GÉANT
le dernier rôle de James Dean

Leslie, de son côté, avait vite été séduite par la franchise, la vigueur, le charme un peu rude de Bick. Tout les séparait, en vérité : les goûts, les habitudes, l'éducation... Mais ils s'aimaient et se marièrent, et Bick ramena fièrement sa jeune épouse au ranch. Sa sœur, Luz, les accueillit froidement.

Luz avait jusqu'alors été la maîtresse incontestée de Reata et n'entendait pas renoncer à ce rôle. Elle avait toujours espéré que son frère épouserait une fille des environs qu'il lui aurait été facile de dominer. Mais la fine, fragile et douce Leslie la déconcertait. Et celle-ci, dépaysée, se demandait comment elle pourrait vivre dans ce pays brutal.

En l'absence de Bick, c'était Jeff Rink, l'intendant, qui avait aidé Luz à diriger le ranch. →

7

Jimmy practiced a "quick-draw" technique for "Giant" as sedulously as he practiced everything for his art . . .

. . . but caught off-guard, as in this picture, he seemed to be sort of smiling at himself. . . .

on the ground carefully examining the underside of the motorcycle.

"I didn't touch you," I said.

"You could have," he answered. "That your car?"

"Yeah," I answered. There was something compelling about his narrow, moody face and his uneven, sandy hair. Very photogenic, I thought professionally.

He scrambled to his feet, walked over to my car and lifted up the hood in a thoroughly experienced manner. I could tell he knew cars.

"Nice," he said earnestly, his head buried deep in the mechanism. "Very nice." He stood up and broke into a big grin. "Want to trade for the motorcycle?"

That was how it began. As far as I was concerned,

Jimmy was just another one of the bluejean brigade of out-of-work actors, only maybe a little more off-beat. He never told me any different.

We used to meet pretty regularly at Googie's for hamburgers and coffee and talk about sports cars and motorcycles. He never talked about his career. I never asked him.

That's one of the first rules of etiquette in Holly-wood. You never ask an actor what he's doing at the moment. If he's working, he'll usually tell you before you get around to asking; if he isn't, the answer you'll generally get is "I'm in between pictures"—which is just a delicate way of saying, "I'm out of work."

I remember having coffee with him one night. The following day I was scheduled to shoot a picture

*Left: Jimmy as Jett Rink being visited at his shack
by the boss's wife – Elizabeth Taylor as Leslie Benedict.
'Giant' was the first movie in which Dean had to play
alongside really big-name stars.*

*legendary in Hollywood. Things did not improve
when he turned up for a pre-production and press
party in a filthy mood. One of the reporters at the
party recalls:*
'He just stared at his boots. When a photographer came close to photograph him, he
quickly put on his dark sunglasses.'

*When a photographer complained that Jimmy was
being uncooperative, Jimmy defended himself.*
'I didn't mean to be rude. It's just that I've
got bags under my eyes, and I need a shave.'

*But Jimmy's apology did nothing to placate
a furious studio representative who had witnessed
the scene.*
'That's typical of the guy. I hope the
Army drafts him and teaches him a little
cooperation.'

*But the probable reason for Jimmy's behaviour
lay with the fact that he was still filming* Rebel
*and had been up all night shooting the scenes
which take place after dark. At this time he would
often have to work through the night and was
exhausted.*
'I haven't slept for two days – no wait, three
days, three nights, that's it.' – *Jimmy Dean*

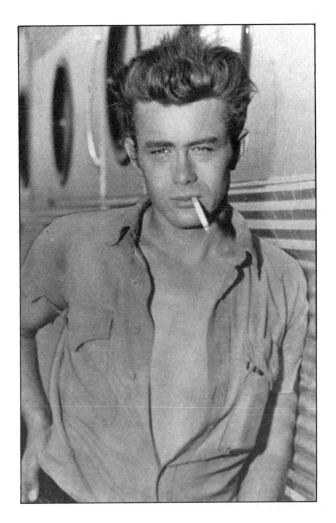

*There was no let-up in Jimmy's gruelling
work schedule. By the end of May, the entire cast
and crew of* Giant *were ensconced in the middle
of the Texan desert to film the outdoor scenes. The
action of the film centres on the Reata Ranch
in deepest Texas – home of wealthy landowner Bick
Benedict (Rock Hudson) and his pretty new
Virginian wife, Leslie (Elizabeth Taylor). Enter
Jimmy Dean as the surly, obstinate cowhand who
is loathed by Bick but loved by his imposing sister
Luz (Mercedes McCambridge) who leaves him
ten acres of scrubland when she is killed in a tragic
riding accident. These ten acres turn out to
be the most valuable land on the whole ranch
when oil is discovered and overnight the humble
cow-poke is transformed into an oil baron. For the
part of Jett Rink, Jimmy had to make a swift and
bold transition from Jim Stark – the mixed-up city*

*delinquent he had just finished playing – to Texan
hick with a soft spot for hard drink and powerful
women. He wrote on his script above the name Jett
Rink:*
'That's me, that's me because I convince
myself that it will be me, really me.' – *Jimmy
Dean*

'Change is the nature of genius.' – *Jimmy
Dean*

*To get into his part, Jimmy started to dress in
typical cowboy clothes – boots, denim shirt, Levis
and a ten gallon hat – which he never took off
either on or off the set. When actress Jane Withers,
who noticed that Jimmy hadn't changed his shirt
for two weeks, offered to wash it for him, he
replied:*

'Thank you, ma'am, but I like it the way it is.'
– *Jimmy Dean*

But Jimmy was just trying to empathise with the character of Jett.

'An actor should thoroughly understand the character he is portraying. There's no better way than trying to be that person in the house, away from the camera. I developed a programme of understanding Jett Rink and doing the things he'd be likely to do. I didn't want any jarring notes in my characterisation. Jett was a victim of his position in life and I wanted to play him sympathetically.' – *Jimmy Dean*

He also spent a lot of time with his dialogue coach,

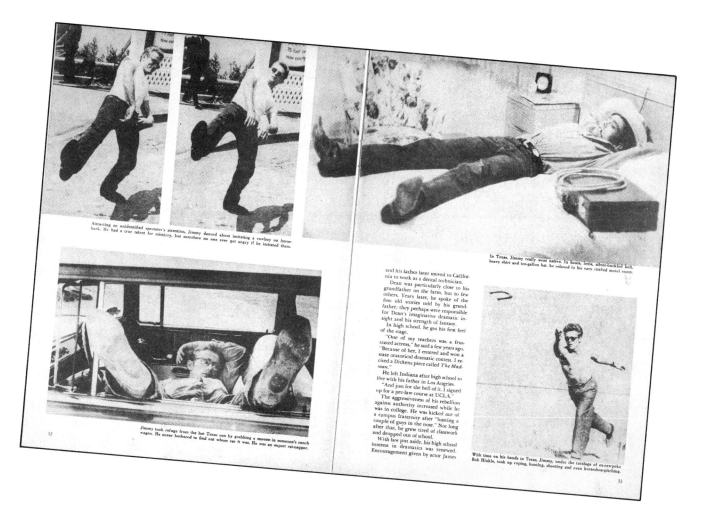

Attracting an unidentified spectator's attention, Jimmy danced about imitating a cowboy on horseback. He had a true talent for mimicry, but somehow no one ever got angry if he imitated them.

In Texas, Jimmy really went native. In boots, levis, silver-buckled belt, heavy shirt and ten-gallon hat, he relaxed in his very citified motel room.

Jimmy took refuge from the hot Texas sun by grabbing a snooze in someone's ranch wagon. He never bothered to find out whose car it was. He was an expert cat-napper.

and his father later moved to California to work as a dental technician.

Dean was particularly close to his grandfather on the farm, but to few others. Years later, he spoke of the fine old stories told by his grandfather; they perhaps were responsible for Dean's imaginative dramatic insight and his strength of fantasy.

In high school, he got his first feel of the stage.

"One of my teachers was a frustrated actress," he said a few years ago. "Because of her, I entered and won a state oratorical dramatic contest. I recited a Dickens piece called *The Madman.*"

He left Indiana after high school to live with his father in Los Angeles.

"And just for the hell of it, I signed up for a pre-law course at UCLA."

The aggressiveness of his rebellion against authority increased while he was in college. He was kicked out of a campus fraternity after "busting a couple of guys in the nose." Not long after that, he grew tired of classwork and dropped out of school.

With law put aside, his high school interest in dramatics was renewed. Encouragement given by actor James

With time on his hands in Texas, Jimmy, under the tutelage of ex-cowpoke Bob Hinkle, took up roping, hunting, shooting and even horseshoe-pitching.

52

53

Bob Hinckle who helped him perfect his Texan drawl.

'They got me a real Texan so that I can learn to talk proper like. Got to learn to ride and rope, too.' – *Jimmy Dean*

The pair would also creep out at night to hunt jack rabbits – real cowboy style. On one of these midnight trips they managed to shoot a coyote – but Jimmy felt mildly uncomfortable about his action and tried to justify it.

'If we hadn't gotten the coyote, it would have killed that lamb. Sure as shooting it would have killed that lamb.' – *Jimmy Dean*

These nocturnal exploits meant that Jimmy would sometimes turn up on the set dog-tired, which didn't impress George Stevens. In fact there

were many who began to resent Jimmy's egocentric behaviour, especially Rock Hudson who didn't like the way Jimmy would try to steal the show.

'He was rough to do a scene with for reasons only an actor can appreciate. While doing a scene, in the giving and taking, he was just a taker. He would suck everything out and never give back.' – *Rock Hudson*

'He was nasty, mean, I don't know what was eating him. If I said hello or good morning he snarled at me.' – *Rock Hudson*

'Once I got ready to shoot an outdoor sequence and I saw a red convertible parked in the middle of a herd of cattle. I didn't have to be told, I knew it was Jimmy.' – *George Stevens*

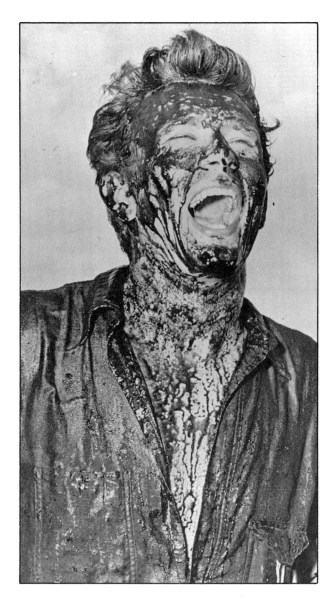

patted. He was the runt in the litter of thoroughbreds. You could feel the loneliness beating out of him, and it hit you like a wave. You can forgive a lot of things for talent and Jimmy was bursting with it.' – *Mercedes McCambridge*

But Jimmy's unease wasn't just to do with hurt pride. He was genuinely in awe of working with such major talents – and for the first time on an open set with hundreds of spectators milling around. When a reporter came up and asked him how he felt he was coping, his reply was disarmingly frank.
'Today my emotional apparatus won't do it. I don't know, plugged up or something – I'm wrenching and punching and packing something. It's not kinda easy for me.' – *Jimmy Dean*

In the first scene Jimmy had to shoot with Elizabeth Taylor he was so nervous that his performance was uninspiring and wooden.
'They did take after take, and it just wasn't going right. He was really getting fucked up. Really nervous. Suddenly he walked away from the set toward a football field where all those people were standing. He wasn't relating to them or anything. He just walked over, he stood there, unzipped his pants, pulled out his cock and took a piss. Then he put his cock back, zipped up his pants, walked back to the set and said, "Okay, shoot". And they did that scene in one take.
 'On the way back from location, I said, "Jimmy, I've seen you do some way out things before, but what was *that*?"
 ' "I was nervous," he said. "I'm a Method actor. I work through my senses. If you're nervous, your senses can't reach your subconscious and that's that – you just can't work. So I figured if I could piss in front of those two thousand people, man, and I could be cool, I figured if I could do that, I could get in front of that camera and do just anything, anything at all." ' – *Dennis Hopper, who played Bick's son, Jordy Benedict, in* Giant

'I'd get so mad at him, and he'd stand there, blinking behind his glasses after having been guilty of some preposterous behaviour, and revealing by his very cast of defiance that he felt some sense of unworthiness. Yet the very next second the glasses would come off, a smile flashes and his whole being is transformed. You were disturbed by him. Now you are dedicated to him.' – *George Stevens*

One of Jimmy's problems was that he was no longer the star of the show. He had to take a seat in the back row in deference to the Hollywood superstar status of characters like Hudson, Taylor and Stevens – a position he found difficult to deal with.
'I can't tell you how he needed to be

"Being a good actor
isn't easy. Being
a man is even harder. I
want to be both . . .
and I will before I'm done."

THE LITTLE THINGS THAT MADE A
MYTH

■ No person ever really knows another. Not completely. Sometimes it seems as if no one really even knows himself. We've heard what his friends, his acquaintances, thought about Jimmy; but we know that despite their best intentions they're not telling the complete truth. They can't. They don't know it. Neither do we. Neither did Jimmy.

His work is the main thing we know of him. It has been left to us and is our heritage. But there are other things, some almost trifling, through which we can remember him, and try to understand him. They're the trivial stories of day to day life, when Jimmy was funny, or sad, or even a good healthy pain-in-the-neck to his friends and co-workers. You see, he wasn't Superman. He was just Jimmy Dean.

For example, Jimmy refused. . . .

■ Jimmy refused to plan anything. He hated schedules, being at certain places at certain times. This quirk is said to be the reason he was late so often on the set. He ignored photographers' instructions on pictures. He said, "You guys, don't you understand that when you shoot a posed subject, you get a posed picture?" If the photographer would stand back a few feet and make some attempt to be inconspicuous, Jimmy would let him shoot pictures indefinitely. He didn't care when the shutter clicked as long as the shots were candid.

"He was a spontaneous person and he loved spontaneous people," says Hollywood photographer Gene Howard.

Jimmy's trouble with directors, both in television and the movies, was over a thing he called "acting space."

"A director should be an intelligent and competent *guide* for the actor," Jimmy often pointed out to other actors. "When an actor plays a scene exactly the way a director orders, it isn't acting. It's following instruction. Anyone with the physical qualifications can do that. So the director's task is just that, to direct, to point the way. Then the actor must take over. And he must be allowed the space, the freedom, to express himself in the role. Without that space an actor is no more than an unthinking robot with a chestful of push-buttons."

Once when asked what he thought of the University of California at Los Angeles (UCLA) where he studied drama, Jimmy answered: "Too many directors and not enough actors."

■ Jimmy's favorite drink was milk. Although he would sip Scotch at a party he preferred imported beers such as Tuborg or Guiness.

When ordering beer in restaurants, cautious maitre d's would frequently ask to see his ID card or some other proof that he was 21. Dean would fumble for his wallet, take it out, hold it up high and let it fall open. From it a cascade of cards, passes, etc., would come down like those long, folding postcards. Jimmy would look at the string of cards, then he would say to the maitre d', "Anything there you like?"

■ One of Jimmy's favorite doodles was a sketch, always a bird's-eye view, of himself in a coffin. And he frequently drew skulls and crossbones.

When Bob Francis was killed in the plane crash, he was the second movie star to die in that cycle of three. The following Sunday Jimmy was having his favorite breakfast, steak and scrambled egg (easy), with a friend. The friend was reading the paper and said to Dean, "Well, Francis makes two."

"Don't worry, I'll be the third," Jimmy commented.

A number of unconnected sources claim that Jim, in commenting on life would often say, "Live young, die young and be a good-looking corpse." However, that line, or one very similar to it, is from "Knock On Any Door," directed by Jim's friend, Nick Ray.

One girl to whom he was introduced said, "He was so intense, when you asked him, 'How are you?' . . . he was stuck for an answer."

But Jimmy wasn't always so intense. He was a gagster too, given to constructing elaborate routines to amuse his friends and mystify "squares."

■ Once, during his New York days, while sitting in Cromwell's, a drugstore and actors' hangout, someone came in excitedly and said, "Isn't it great about Biff Elliot! He just got the lead in that Spillane film." It seemed to Jimmy that within seconds everyone in the drugstore had repeated the words, "Isn't it great about Biff Elliot!" Something about this amused Jimmy, so he turned to his friend Marty Landau and said, "Isn't it great about Merv Paine!" He found that if he said it with enough conviction, he'd convince everyone in the store that it really was great, the most wonderful thing in the world. Of course, there was no such person as Merv Paine. Nevertheless, weeks later, Jimmy enjoyed hearing people come up to him and say: "Did you hear about Merv Paine? Isn't it the greatest!"

"Merv Paine" became a watchword between Jimmy and Marty. If Jimmy met someone who he felt was a dead-head, he would say to Marty: "You know, this fellow reminds me of Merv Paine." It was his secret way of saying that the guy was nobody.

Jimmy enjoyed a stunt in which he would walk over a sidewalk grating, make a great "swooshing" sound and lift his overcoat over his head. Marty, who was walking about ten feet behind him, would run up. "Good Grief! What was that?" Marty would scream. "I don't know! I don't know!" Jimmy would cry. "It came from down there. I think some-

"the actor must take over"

thing's about to explode." When a sufficiently huge crowd had gathered and the braver ones were trying to work up their nerve to approach the grating, Jimmy and Marty would steal away, cross the street and watch the excitement from there. "Some bunch, aren't they?" Jimmy would say, smiling broadly.

-The boys, for some reason, spent a great deal of time at an ice skating rink, just standing and cheering on an inexpressibly bad skater. Nevertheless she was a young lady of extraordinarily good looks, and every time she skated by on her ankles the boys would break into raucous cheers and applause. She obviously liked it, since she continued to return nightly for six months. Her skating never improved, nor did she ever meet her admirers.

■ Jimmy was a very impatient man. Desire sprang in his breast quickly and whenever such hot "wants" developed he would neglect everything else—his work, his appointments. Nothing mattered for the moment except the satisfaction of the yearning.

On a visit to Photographer Sanford Roth's home a few months before his death, he became fascinated with Mrs. Roth's wide knowledge of cats. Jimmy said he'd like to have a cat. Mrs. Roth recommended a Siamese or a Burmese breed. From the pictures, Jimmy decided it was a Burmese he wanted.

"Where do they sell them?" he asked.

"In Idlewyld," answered Mrs. Roth. (Idlewyld is near San Bernardino, about 80 miles from Hollywood.)

"Let's go get one," said Jimmy.

"Now?" said Mrs. Roth.

"Now!" said Jimmy. It was difficult to talk him out of it.

MORE

Jimmy was finding that his hopes for the role of Jett Rink were meeting with many disappointments. First, he did not have the understanding of some of the other actors when it came to his rather idiosyncratic method of preparing for a scene.

'Before coming on set he used to warm up like a fighter before a contest. He never stepped into camera range without first jumping into the air with his knees up under his chin, or running at full speed around the set shrieking like a bird of prey.' – *Rock Hudson*

He also discovered soon enough that Stevens' own methods of making a film, which involved numerous takes of the same scene, did not fit in with his own acting technique, which relied far more heavily on spur-of-the-moment inspiration. Jimmy complained to Bill Bast:

Left: 'The James Dean Anniversary Book' used an image from 'Giant' for its profile of Dean. Left below: Jimmy as the ageing Jett Rink. Below: After initial hostility, gossip supremo Hedda Hopper became one of his supporters.

'They show up at the beginning of a day's shooting without any real plan. Somehow they sort of muddle through. Stevens has a method I call the "round the clock" system. He takes all that film and shoots every scene from every possible angle – all round the scene, up, down, here, there – and when he's through he gets himself the best editor in town. Then they spend a year selecting from miles and miles of film the best shots and the best scenes. They figure the whole thing out like a jigsaw puzzle. And when they're through, surprise! – another masterpiece. How can he go wrong?' – *Jimmy Dean*

The biggest irritation with this way of working for Jimmy was the time factor. Often he would be called to the set, made-up and ready to go, and would have to wait for hours while Stevens got all the shots he could possibly want from the scene already in progress. For the first time in

his life the tables were turned and it was Jimmy Dean who was forced to kick his heels while his colleague spent all the time he wanted perfecting his creation. This so riled him that occasionally he wouldn't bother to turn up to rehearsals on time if he didn't think he would be needed until later. Predictably, he couldn't judge it accurately and a whole morning was wasted back at the Hollywood studios looking for him around town when he was meant to be on set. Stevens and the Warners management did not hold back their fury when he finally turned up, but Jimmy snarled back.
'Are you finished? Well, let me tell *you* something. I may be working in a factory, but I'm not a machine. I stayed up all night Friday to do that scene. I prepared all night for that scene. I came in ready to work and you kept me sitting around all day. Do you realise I'm doing emotional memories? That I'm working with my senses – my sight, hearing, smell, touch? Can I tell you that

*Hollywood columnist **Hedda** Hopper was one of James Dean's most ardent fans. From the very start of his movie career, she was the only member of the press corps who managed to break through the barrier around Jimmy and find out what he was really like. Because of Hedda's deep affection for Jimmy, we thought you might like to read what she wrote about him in her Motion Picture Magazine columns over a 20-month period.*

November, 1954: Though Pier Angeli's mama was upset over Pier's romance with James Dean, she ended up cooking dinners for him. Jimmy's one of the Dirty Shirttail group of actors—he didn't own a tuxedo, so he borrowed one to take Pier out.
February, 1955: James Dean lost out to Vic Damone in his romance with Pier Angeli, but those who've seen his first picture, *East of Eden*, claim he's the newest star on the Hollywood horizon. This young lad turned down the lead in *The Egyptian* when Marlon Brando walked out. He insisted on doing his first picture for director Elia Kazan. Evidently it paid off.
March, 1955: I didn't see him, but I'm told that James Dean, who courted Pier Angeli up to the minute she announced her engagement to Vic Damone, sat outside the church on his motorcycle while she got married. He has since switched his motorcycle for a German sports car—the latest thing in swank. And he's dated Vampira a couple of times. Perhaps he was just scouting cartoon material for Charles Addams. He is sensational, sullen and seductive and is Holly-
[*Please turn to page 60*]

Jimmy Dean didn't especially like reporters, but he and Hedda Hopper became good friends and she often visited him on the set. Here, the famed columnist chats with Jim in his dressing room between scenes on Giant.

For Jimmy, Hedda was... A FAN, A FRIEND, A FIGHTER

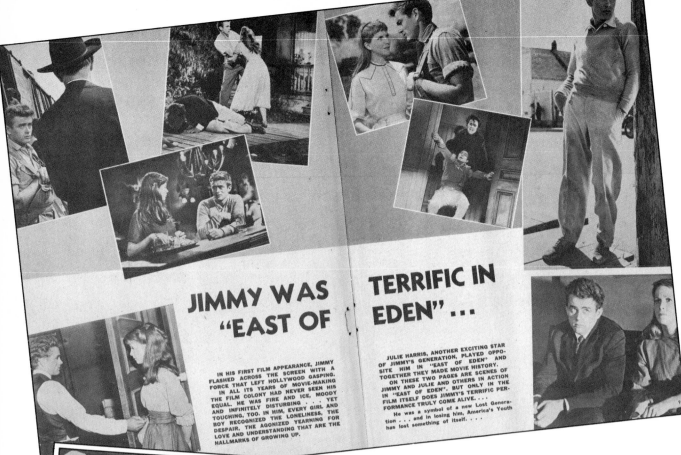

JIMMY WAS TERRIFIC IN "EAST OF EDEN" ...

IN HIS FIRST FILM APPEARANCE, JIMMY FLASHED ACROSS THE SCREEN WITH A FORCE THAT LEFT HOLLYWOOD GASPING. IN ALL ITS YEARS OF MOVIE-MAKING THE FILM COLONY HAD NEVER SEEN HIS EQUAL. HE WAS FIRE AND ICE, MOODY AND INFINITELY DISTURBING . . . YET TOUCHING, TOO. IN HIM, EVERY GIRL AND BOY RECOGNIZED THE LONELINESS, THE DESPAIR, THE AGONIZED YEARNING FOR LOVE AND UNDERSTANDING THAT ARE THE HALLMARKS OF GROWING UP.

JULIE HARRIS, ANOTHER EXCITING STAR OF JIMMY'S GENERATION, PLAYED OPPO-SITE HIM IN "EAST OF EDEN" AND TOGETHER THEY MADE MOVIE HISTORY. ON THESE TWO PAGES ARE SCENES OF JIMMY AND JULIE AND OTHERS IN ACTION IN "EAST OF EDEN". BUT ONLY IN THE FILM ITSELF DOES JIMMY'S TERRIFIC PER-FORMANCE TRULY COME ALIVE....

He was a symbol of a new Lost Genera-tion . . . and in losing him, America's Youth has lost something of itself. . . .

AND IN "REBEL WITHOUT A CAUSE" HE WAS EVEN BETTER...

IN HIS SECOND FILM, "REBEL WITHOUT A CAUSE", JIMMY ROSE TO NEW HEIGHTS OF ACTING GLORY. NOW HE WAS A MISUNDERSTOOD YOUTH—AND HE GAVE TO HIS INTERPRETATION OF THE ROLE SUCH A DRIVING INTENSITY THAT EVERYONE WHO WITNESSED IT WAS EMOTIONALLY SHAKEN . . . ALL OVER THE WORLD, JIM-MY'S NAME AND FAME WERE BECOMING A HOUSEHOLD WORD, HIS TECHNIQUE WIDELY IMITATED. . . .

for every day you make me sit, there'll be two days next time? Then three, then four? You'll pay for it. And you're not going to stop me from working. Now let's get back to the set.'
– *Jimmy Dean*

Jimmy also voiced his anger at this treatment to Hedda Hopper.
'Stevens has been horrible. I sat there for three days, made-up and ready to work at nine o'clock every morning. By six o'clock I hadn't had a scene or a rehearsal. I sat there like a bump on a log watching that big lumpy Rock Hudson making love to Liz Taylor. I

knew what Stevens was trying to do to me.'
– *Jimmy Dean*

There was a lot of friction between Jimmy and Stevens about the way the role of Jett Rink should be played. Stevens, unlike Nick Ray, was an old-fashioned, autocratic director who expected actors to act while he made the creative decisions. This was a huge blow for Jimmy, who was bursting with ideas and suggestions, most of which were tacitly ignored. He became hugely frustrated about the way his part was shaping up.
'That sort of frustration is real heavy to carry. How to handle an individual, that's what

Below: It was not only the show-business or teen magazines like 'Picturegoer' (right) that gave prominence to Jimmy's posthumous career, but also the up-market monthlies like 'Look' magazine (below).

Jimmy Dean was killed in an automobile accident last year, but hundreds of thousands of fans all over the world still write to him.

What is the explanation of this strange posthumous fame?

James Dean
THE LEGEND AND THE FACTS

By GEORGE SCULLIN

That change first became evident at Warner Bros. along about the first of this year. Back in September of 1955, they had lost James Dean in an automobile accident, and for a few weeks, the office had been swamped with letters, a large portion of which expressed an almost hysterical resentment at an untimely death. Then had followed a lull which Hollywood has come to recognize as the prelude to obscurity. Instead, December saw an upsurge in the volume of mail, and a change in the tenor of the contents. January brought in more than 3,000 letters with requests for photographs, graphs of Dean. By the end of July, when requests for photographs with payments enclosed, had risen to 7,800 for the month, there could no longer be any doubt. This was not a requiem to a dead star. It was a tribute to a living legend.

This mass demonstration of hero worship baffled even the press agents, for it was not their work, but it didn't take the "fringe" interests long to get aboard. Magazines devoted exclusively to the life of James Dean sell out hundreds of thousands of copies on publication. Curio and book shops discovered that photographs of Dean outsell all the other stars of Hollywood history. A sculptured head of Dean is a 'hot item' at $30. There is a life mask of Dean in the Laurence Hutton collection at Princeton University, along with masks of Garrick and Booth, Thackeray and Keats, Beethoven and other immortals. Television stations average thousands of letters a month demanding repeats of Dean's few TV appearances. A Forest record, *His Name Was Dean*, sold 25,000 copies its first week of sale.

Alienists describe this wave of posthumous adulation as morbid, strange, mystic, cultist or just plain unhealthy. But any psychiatrist—and all parents of teen-agers are psychiatrists by necessity—could explain the phenomenon with one hand tied behind him:

In the complicated psyche of the growing boy or girl, two im-
continued

Dean posed for LOOK against this grotesque background of his own choice not long before his death.

Giant, his third and last picture, will be released this month. That's Elizabeth Taylor, roped and happy.

Hollywood is all about. If you're run-of-the-mill, if you can sing so that housewives think they can sing in the bathtub as well as you can, then you're in. Or if you look just about the average face, then okay. But if you're very beautiful or if you're looking for the individual inside of yourself in order to act at all, if you're very different – then there's frustration. What they need is a stuffed doll. I think it's all that Hollywood can handle.' – *Jimmy Dean*

'Dammit, I know I'm a much better actor than what's being done with me at the moment. I'm being inhibited, restricted, I'm not able to exercise the full capacity of my abilities.' – *Jimmy Dean*

'Sometimes he broke a scene down into so many bits and pieces that I couldn't see the scene for the trees, so as to speak. I must admit that I sometimes underestimated him; and sometimes he overestimated the effects he thought he was getting. Then he might change his approach, do it quick, and if that didn't work we'd effect a compromise. All in all it was a hell of a headache to work with him. He was always pulling and hauling, and he had developed this cultivated, designed irresponsibility. It's tough on you, he'd seem to imply, but I've just got to do it this way. From the director's angle that isn't the most delightful sort of fellow to work with.' – *George Stevens*

'I don't even want to see the picture. That's not me, that's not where I want to go. Stevens isn't helping me mature the character of Jett Rink – not in the way the character should have matured and grown to become the character at the end of the picture that was needed.' – *Jimmy Dean*

'I hate pictures and Stevens is no better than the others. Only he can't go wrong. Do you know he gets more footage, more film, than anybody else at Warner Brothers?' – *Jimmy Dean*

'It was really depressing to see the suffering that boy was going through. *Giant* was really draining him, and I hated watching it happen.' – *Nick Ray*

Even Stevens himself admitted much later that he should have paid more attention to Jimmy's innate understanding of the role:
'Whenever I do a film, I always feel that I know the characters and the actor is just acquainted with them, because I have the whole script and relate to the whole thing. I had one scene with Jimmy – when the Benedicts give this big party for Leslie – and I told Jimmy, ''Go over toward her and as you pass the bar, pour yourself a big drink and drink it down. Pour yourself another one if you like.'' And he said to me, ''Look, I

DONOVAN PEDELTY REPORTING FROM HOLLYWOOD

A GIANT OF A PREMIÈRE

This headline told you ("Picturegoer," December 1) how Hollywood greeted James Dean's final picture. Now we add

AND IT'S A GIANT OF A FILM

Elizabeth Taylor and Rock Hudson both give superb performances

The performance of Dean is amusing, tricksy, but at odds with the atmosphere

GIANT ★★★★

| | ELIZABETH TAYLOR | ROCK HUDSON | JAMES DEAN |

IF this doesn't drag people away from their TV sets, nothing will! Rarely before has so much sheer entertainment been combined with such a genuine mastery of film-making. A PICTUREGOER Seal Of Merit film, of course. I only wish I could double the honour!

At heart the loosely woven story from Edna Ferber's novel is a family " births, marriages and deaths " chronicle. The giant is Texas: the young, sprawling, materialistic state, vastly different from the sedate, tradition-ridden Maryland home of the heroine (Elizabeth Taylor).

A young Texan visitor (Rock Hudson), in the twenties, sweeps her off her feet and back to his mammoth cattle ranch as his wife.

There an unfamiliar world awaits her: a ruthless, raw world, where delicacy and graciousness are unknown. Her husband cannot understand her revulsion.

Through the years—and through her children's eyes—she sees this world change. The hired hand (James Dean) becomes rich, ruthless and respected when oil is discovered on the tiny patch of land he inherited.

Texas gives itself a veneer of glamour and sophistication, but the racial tensions—between whites and Mexicans—and the gross vulgarity continue to bubble away beneath the surface.

At first the treatment seems slow. But the slowness pays off in the depth of characterization and the breadth of meaning in each carefully composed shot. Not a moment of the three and a half hours' running time seems wasted.

The surprise of the film is to watch Rock Hudson roundly out-act Dean, whose performance proves to be amusing, subtle, tricksy, but completely at odds with the atmosphere of the film.

Hudson, however, grows and develops with it. Elizabeth Taylor gives a maturing, delicate characterization.

The rest of the cast, from Mercedes McCambridge as Hudson's bitter, tight-lipped sister, to Carroll Baker, Dennis Hopper and Fran Bennett as his three children, is about perfect.

There's a whale of a performance from Jane Withers as a Texas matron.

Leslie Benedict .... ELIZABETH TAYLOR
Bick Benedict .. ROCK HUDSON
Jett Rink .... JAMES DEAN
Vashti Snythe ... JANE WITHERS
Uncle Bawley ... CHILL WILLS
Luz Benedict .... MERCEDES McCAMBRIDGE
Luz Benedict II .... CARROLL BAKER
Jordon Benedict III .... DENNIS HOPPER
Dr. Horace Lynnton PAUL FIX
Mrs. Lynnton JUDITH EVELYN
Sir David .... RODNEY TAYLOR

WARNER BROS. AMERICAN. "A." 197 MINUTES. WARNERCOLOR. PRODUCED BY GEORGE STEVENS AND HENRY GINSBERG. DIRECTOR: GEORGE STEVENS. PHOTOGRAPHED BY WILLIAM C. MELLOR. MUSIC: DIMITRI TIOMKIN. SCREENPLAY: FRED GUIOL, IVAN MOFFAT. BASED ON THE NOVEL BY EDNA FERBER. RELEASE: MARCH 24.

STARS IN YOUR EYES c ★

| | NAT JACKLEY | PAT KIRKWOOD | BONAR COLLEANO |

THE moral here seems to be that Variety isn't dead. But, if it isn't yet, this itsy-bitsy musical may be the mortal blow. Not that it lacks talent.

Pat Kirkwood has the warmth and the whoosh and needs only the part. Nat Jackley may not be everyone's comic, but he has some of the stuff of the old-style Variety.

Bonar Colleano, both as an entertainer and an actor, has always seemed to me sadly under-rated. And, on the side, Dorothy Squires, Hubert Gregg and Jack Jackson lend their talents liberally.

The film, though, never really gets off the ground. The plot is old but still serviceable: out - of - work artists putting on their own show, taking the knocks and finally—success!

But the laughs are thin, the routines too routine and the production needs a lot more genuine zip.

Too bad, because the energy everyone puts into it would power a battleship—yes, even in this atomic age!

Jimmy Knowles NAT JACKLEY
Sally Bishop .. PAT KIRKWOOD
David Laws BONAR COLLEANO
Ann Hart .. DOROTHY SQUIRES
Rigby .... JACK JACKSON
Maureen Temple ... VERA DAY
Crawley Walters .... HUBERT GREGG
Walters's secretary JOAN SIMS
Ronnie .... RONNIE CLARK
Dicky .... GERALD HARPER
Maxie Jago MEIER TZELNIKER
Effie .... GABRIELLE BRUNE

BRITISH LION. GRAND ALLIANCE. BRITISH. CAMERASCOPE. "U." 96 MINS. EASTMAN COLOUR. PRODUCER: DAVID DENT. DIRECTOR: MAURICE ELVEY. PHOTOGRAPHED BY S. D. ONIONS. MUSIC DIRECTED BY EDWIN ASTLEY. SCREENPLAY: TALBOT ROTHWELL. RELEASE: NOT FIXED.

"I see you walking down the aisle and you're carrying . . ." "Orchids!" "No, dear, a choc ice and a one and nine ticket"

Left: Dean as Jett, setting up the initial oil derrick on his land. There are many sequences in 'Giant' which feature Dean by himself, which reveal a new maturity developing in his acting style.

have this flask in my pocket. Why don't I go over to the bar and get a glass and pour the stuff from my flask?'' And I said, ''Forget it, Jimmy. It's *their* booze. Pour yourself a big drink of *their* stuff.''

'And I realised a few years ago, that what Jimmy wanted to do would have been the cutest bit in the movie. His point was that it had to do with pride – he was too *proud* to take a drink from their table. Usually I think I know a character better than anyone, but what I told Jimmy was damn wrong. His idea was too damn smart, and he didn't explain it to me, so I didn't get it then. But he really knew that character, and that's the best tribute I can pay to his talent as an actor.' – *George Stevens*

'He was too good for it. Anybody could have played that part.' – *George Stevens*

But in spite of Jimmy's grave misgivings about the characterisation, his performance received much acclaim when the film was finally released in October 1956 – a year after his death – and he was posthumously nominated for an Oscar.
'James Dean was a genius. I don't think there's another actor in the world who could have portrayed Jett as well as he. But like most geniuses, Dean suffered from success poisoning.' – *Edna Ferber, who wrote the novel* Giant

Jimmy was being accused of 'success poisoning' by many others by the time Giant *was in its final stages of shooting in Hollywood in September 1955.*
'He was a neurotic, mixed-up kid who tried to con everybody to death. There just wasn't an ounce of maturity in that boy.' – *Alec Wilder, composer*

'He was surly, ill-tempered, brutal without any element of kindness, sensitivity, consideration for others, or romantic passion. He was physically dirty. He hated to bathe, have his hair cut, shave, or put on clean

Below: The original novel of 'Giant' was reissued with Dean on the cover. Bottom: Although he and Dean had not got on, director George Stevens wrote a sympathetic appreciation in 'Modern Screen', January 1956.

GIANT

FOUR SQUARE BOOKS

A mighty story of a mighty state—Texas
'A real bombshell of a novel'—Alan Melville, B.B.C.

EDNA FERBER

3/6

Elizabeth Taylor, Rock Hudson and the late James Dean in Warner Brothers' film 'Giant'

clothes. He smelled so rankly that actresses working in close contact with him found him unbearable.' – *Maurice Zolotov, novelist*

'He loved being a star. He adored that attention and he wanted it desperately, I felt. But it mattered so much that he almost had to treat it with contempt. He couldn't admit how much it meant to him.' – *Carroll Baker, who co-starred with Jimmy in* Giant.

Jimmy blamed much of this 'success poisoning' on plain, simple exhaustion.
'The trouble is with me I'm just dog-tired, everybody hates me and thinks I'm a heel. They say I've gone Hollywood, but honest I'm just the same as when I didn't have

by George Stevens

For nearly two decades tall, affable George Stevens has been a force for artistry in Hollywood. From Gunga Din to A Place In The Sun he has contributed some of the best movies we have had. At this moment he is putting the finishing touches to his latest picture, Edna Ferber's Giant, starring Elizabeth Taylor, Rock Hudson and the late James Byron Dean, of whom he wrote this moving story.

■ I spent six hours today with Jimmy Dean, as I have most of the days in these past two months. He is always up there on the projection-room screen in front of me, challenging me not to like any part of him in the picture. And there is no part of Jimmy I don't like, no part of him that hasn't always the attraction that goes with complete naturalness. Maybe it is the way he sidles next to someone, chin hugging his chest, then squints up out of the corner of his eye, mumbling a greeting. Or maybe the way he can run a boyish giggle right through his words or, without losing an iota of expressiveness, violate all the dramatic precepts and persistently present only his back to the camera.

When there is this much distinction and force to a personality you can't believe it can ever be destroyed. Certainly for me, as I put together his last picture, Giant, the Dean who drove to his death on a cool September evening in northern California is unreal. The real one is the Jimmy I knew and *(Continued on page 68)*

A TENDERNESS LOST

photo by Roy Schatt

More pictures on the following pages

Left: Dean was not afraid to wear his glasses in public. Below: 'The James Dean Anniversary Book' got quotes from most of the actresses he worked with. Right: Dean with Ursula Andress.

a dime. I went right into *Giant* immediately after a long hard schedule on *Rebel*. Maybe I'd just better go away for a while.' – *Jimmy Dean*

But as always with Jimmy, his crucial underlying problem was his sense of loneliness and as work on Giant *progressed he seemed to be retreating more and more into himself.*
'I wouldn't like me if I had to be around me.' – *Jimmy Dean*

'We were all trying to be individualists in such a devoted way. But I think that Jimmy really didn't have to work at it. I think that he was actually an individualist among a group of individualists. He used to be at parties

AND THOSE WHO KEEP HIS MEMORY BRIGHT

LORI NELSON—"To me, Jimmy was always polite and a little shy. But I was impressed most by his genuine love for animals. Sometimes, watching him stroke a horse's mane, or pat a dog, I felt he possessed that unusual faculty for communicating with animals. You could almost see the mutual trust that existed between them.
"When Jimmy died, the world lost a man who knew kindness. For that alone we should remember him."

KATY JURADO—"Jimmy was the strangest actor I've ever known. He was never the same person you left at the last meeting. He'd be different each time. His knowledge of and love for music, sports cars, acting and art was amazing. He knew every little thing. You could not help but love his spirit.
"When I heard that he had died I thought of many of the young men in my country, Mexico, who cannot resist facing death. They are the matadors. Jimmy understood that bullfighting was not a sport, but an art."

LIZ TAYLOR—"Jimmy and I became close friends during the filming of Giant. I'd heard that he was difficult to work with. I hadn't known him ten minutes when I knew this was not true. Instead Jimmy turned out to be a practical joker, on the set and off.
"I cannot say what I felt on learning of his death, but all of us treasure his memory."

JANE WITHERS—"I joined the cast of Giant after a long absence from the movies. So much had happened. I wasn't sure I could catch up. Then I met Jimmy. He was the most wonderful tease in the world. And he made me laugh. He must have guessed that laughter was what I needed.
"Yes, in the tragedy of his death, I find that remembering him still makes me smile. I think that would please him."

Few women understood Jimmy the way Natalie Wood did. Theirs was a perfect friendship in which Jimmy was free of the torments which characterized so many of his relationships.

WE WHO LIVE ON

20

2

where the other actors were. Never say a word to anyone. If we were listening to music he would sit in the corner and play his bongo drums. And I don't think I ever remember him holding a conversation with anyone. Maybe a few words here and there.' – *Carroll Baker*

'I used to feel that he was a disturbed boy, tremendously dedicated to some intangible beacon of his own, and neither he nor anyone else might ever know what it was. I used to feel this because at times when he fell quiet and thoughtful, as if inner-bidden to dream about something, an odd and unconscious

sweetness would light up his countenance. At such times, and because I knew he had been motherless since early childhood and had missed a lot of love that makes boyhood gel, I would come to believe that he was still waiting for some lost tenderness.' – *George Stevens*

One of the close relationships Jimmy had at this time was with the glamorous European starlet Ursula Andress, whose radical chic was very appealing to him. They had met soon after his return from Texas in the summer of 1955 when she was still a newcomer to Hollywood.
'He came by my house late. He came in room

like wild animal, and smell of everything I don't like. We go hear jazz music and he leave table. Say he go play drums. He no come back. I don't like to be alone. I go home. He come by my home later and say he sorry. Ask if I want to see his motorsickle. We sit on sidewalk in front of motorsickle and talk, talk, talk, until five.' – *Ursula Andress*

But their relationship was based more on physical passion than on mutual understanding.
'Jimmy and Ursula Andress were at a party at Don the Beachcombers, which was next door to the Villa Capri restaurant. And Jimmy asked me to pose with him, since she [Ursula] hadn't had her photo taken with him. But a few minutes later Jimmy was kicked out of the place after he had become boisterous, being as drunk as he was. And when he was asked to leave, his pants were unzipped and apparently Ursula, who didn't speak much English, was communicating to Jimmy in another way.' – *Stephanie Skolsky*

Although Ursula was beautiful and sensuous, she was also intelligent, very independent and fiery and the couple were famous for their arguments.
'We fight like cats and dogs. No, on second thought, like two monsters. But then we make up and it's fun. Ursula doesn't take any baloney from me and I don't take any from her. I guess it's because we're both so egotistical.'– *Jimmy Dean*

One recurring bone of contention was Ursula's expensive tastes.
'It's costing me five dollars every time I take you out. Why can't you eat spaghetti for 65 cents?' – *Jimmy Dean to Ursula Andress*

Jimmy also criticised her for keeping a huge German Shepherd dog, which cost a lot to feed.
'It'd be cheaper to have a family.' – *Jimmy Dean*

After many arguments and break-ups the couple finally split up for good when Ursula went off with John Derrick. Jimmy spent the last few months of his life living alone in a house in the San Fernando Valley, with his new cat, Marcus, for company. Elizabeth Taylor had presented him with the Siamese kitten as a present, hoping that it would provide some company for him.
'One felt he was a boy one had to take care of, but even that was probably his joke. I don't think he needed anybody or anything –

except his acting.' – *Elizabeth Taylor*

Jimmy became very attached to his kitten.
'He's like an electric mixer that until it's
plugged in, it isn't functioning, and with him
until he was feeling close, like in a spiritual
marriage with someone, it didn't matter who,
male or female, young or old, or maybe even
an animal, I don't know but unless he felt
really close, married to someone, he didn't
function. He was just frantic until he found
this feeling of togetherness with someone he
loved and trusted.' – *Vampira*

*Jimmy himself admitted that marriage – spiritual
or otherwise – was something he craved.*
'It would be so right to come home to
somebody who understands me, who cares.'
– *Jimmy Dean*

*He seemed to be losing himself amidst the
impersonal and superficial glitz and glamour of
Hollywood.*
'I really don't know who I am but it really
doesn't matter.' – *Jimmy Dean*

Chapter 7

LIVE FAST, DIE YOUNG

'Death. It's the only thing left to respect.
It's the one immutable, undeniable truth.
Everything else can be questioned. But
death is truth. In it lies the only nobility
for man, and beyond it the only hope.'
Jimmy Dean

'You've got to live fast; death comes early.'
– Jimmy Dean

Jimmy finished his last scene in Giant *on 22 September 1955. It was one of the most difficult scenes of the entire film for him to play since the character of Jett had grown 30 years older and had degenerated into an ineffectual drunk. The final scene leaves Jett incoherent and semi-conscious, slumped drunkenly over the banquet table in a darkened and empty room. Jimmy was relieved to get this gruelling and difficult work over, and was planning to have some time off to relax and enjoy himself. His parting words to George Stevens:* 'Now it's all over, we don't have to bug each other no more. And I can go back to my motor racing.' *– Jimmy Dean*

Jane Deacy was already busy setting up Jimmy's future. She negotiated an incredible fee of $20,000 for a TV epic The Corn Is Green *and was discussing a $900,000 film contract with Warners. His next film role was to play the New York boxer Rocky Graziano, a man for whom Jimmy felt much admiration.*
'What a guy, one day when he was in the army, he got tired of it and just got up – walked out – went over the hill. The army never forgave him…You've got to admire that kind of nerve.' – Jimmy Dean

But before taking on any more work, Jimmy wanted some time to himself, and it was agreed that he could take a year off before he was back on the Hollywood production line once more.

ILLUSTRATED—January 5, 1957

Rebel's ruin. James Dean, with his moustache and middle-aged look as the newly-rich inebriate at the end of his tether, in his new film "Giant"

My challenge to the rebels without a hero—

Find yourselves a real cause

urges GILBERT HARDING

DEAN was a tearaway, in rebellion.   appeal for the young—rightly always   the present time is by no means untinged with glory.
What's wrong with Bader? Or, if

JAMES DEAN'S GREATEST PERFORMANCE

(Continued)

THROUGHOUT the shooting of *Giant* both in Texas and in Hollywood, the set was "open"—that is, reporters and spectators were permitted to watch at any time. But producer Henry Ginsberg and director George Stevens agreed that for one scene the set should be closed, because of its staggering demands upon the actors' talent. When the scene was finished, the only audience—hardened crewmen and technicians—stood silent and shaken, eyes filled with tears. This is the scene.

Returning to the speaker's table, Jett passes out before he can deliver his speech. When he revives, the guests are gone, he is alone in the room.

In his befuddled state he imagines that the people are still there, and his social triumph is at hand. Forcefully, he begins to speak.

Rambling and incoherent, he plunges into the address he had so carefully prepared, his drunken behavior making a mockery of every line.

Unable to go on, he sinks to a chair. Slowly, as his mind begins to clear, he realizes his pitiful failure. Broken and agonized, he tries to fight back at the terrible truth. In a final helpless effort pulls himself together enough to make another lunge at the speaker's mike.

He falls on his face upon the mike and the text that was to win him more than his millions ever could—respect of his followmen. He has lost his girl, Luz Benedict, too. Feeling that her brother and father have ruined Jett's big day, she rushes back to him, only to stop at the door, bitterly disillusioned by seeing him in such a disgraceful state, then turns away to go home to her folks. Thus Jett learns all his riches cannot buy what he needs—love.

'I don't want to burn myself out...I've made three pictures in the last two years.' – *Jimmy Dean*

And Jimmy had plenty of other interests besides acting which fascinated him and which he wanted to pursue further.
'If I live to be a hundred, there won't be time to do everything I want.' – *Jimmy Dean*

He had become increasingly involved in the creative arts as a new source of inspiration and development. He was learning sculpture under the direction of Pegot Waring, and as well as practising the bongo drums and violin, he was always widening his knowledge of music.
'I collect everything from twelfth and thirteenth century music to the extreme moderns – you know, Schoenberg, Berg, Stravinsky. I also like Sinatra's *Songs For Young Lovers* album.' – *Jimmy Dean*

He was also making new friends – not the one-night variety, but more lasting and platonic friendships. One of the most important relation-

ships for Jimmy at this time was with the photographer Sanford Roth and his wife, Beulah. When Jimmy was first introduced to Sandy Roth, he didn't hide his profound admiration for him. 'Are you Sanford H. Roth? Did you do the book on Paris with Aldous Huxley?' – Jimmy Dean

But hero worship developed into mutual respect, and the Roths became Jimmy's closest companions and knew him better than anyone at this time. 'Too often James Dean has been described as a meteor, a crazy mixed-up kid, a Great Dane puppy and a poet. He was all of these and at the same time none. His laugh was a half-silent chuckle, as though exuberance embarrassed him. His enthusiasms ran through the spectrum of human interests; motorcycles, jazz, bull-fighting, apple pie, plum preserves, cats and serious music. I knew little of his personal life. He was the least self-revealing human being I ever met. But he had the austere good sense of a Quaker and the defence

Left: With a year off written into his contract, Jimmy hoped for time to indulge in some of his other interests.

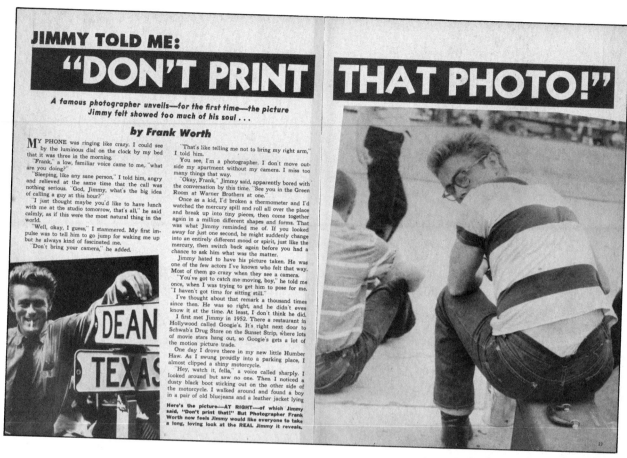

JIMMY TOLD ME:

"DON'T PRINT THAT PHOTO!"

A famous photographer unveils—for the first time—the picture Jimmy felt showed too much of his soul . . .

by Frank Worth

MY PHONE was ringing like crazy. I could see by the luminous dial on the clock by my bed that it was three in the morning.

"Frank," a low, familiar voice came to me, "what are you doing?"

"Sleeping, like any sane person," I told him, angry and relieved at the same time that the call was nothing serious. "God, Jimmy, what's the big idea of calling a guy at this hour?"

"I just thought maybe you'd like to have lunch with me at the studio tomorrow, that's all," he said calmly, as if this were the most natural thing in the world.

"Well, okay, I guess," I stammered. My first impulse was to tell him to go jump for waking me up but he always kind of fascinated me.

"Don't bring your camera," he added.

"That's like telling me not to bring my right arm," I told him.

You see, I'm a photographer. I don't move outside my apartment without my camera. I miss too many things that way.

"Okay, Frank," Jimmy said, apparently bored with the conversation by this time. "See you in the Green Room at Warner Brothers at one."

Once as a kid, I'd broken a thermometer and I'd watched the mercury spill and roll all over the place and break up into tiny pieces, then come together again in a million different shapes and forms. That was what Jimmy reminded me of. If you looked away for just one second, he might suddenly change into an entirely different mood or spirit, just like the mercury, then switch back again before you had a chance to ask him what was the matter.

Jimmy hated to have his picture taken. He was one of the few actors I've known who felt that way. Most of them go crazy when they see a camera.

"You've got to catch me moving, boy," he told me once, when I was trying to get him to pose for me. "I haven't got time for sitting still."

I've thought about that remark a thousand times since then. He was so right, and he didn't even know it at the time. At least, I don't think he did.

I first met Jimmy in 1952. There's a restaurant in Hollywood called Googie's. It's right next door to Schwab's Drug Store on the Sunset Strip, where lots of movie stars hang out, so Googie's gets a lot of the motion picture trade.

One day I drove there in my new little Humber Haw. As I swung proudly into a parking place, I almost clipped a shiny motorcycle.

"Hey, watch it, fella," a voice called sharply. I looked around but saw no one. Then I noticed a dusty black boot sticking out on the other side of the motorcycle. I walked around and found a boy in a pair of old bluejeans and a leather jacket lying

Here's the picture—AT RIGHT—of which Jimmy said, "Don't print that!" But Photographer Frank Worth now feels Jimmy would like everyone to take a long, loving look at the REAL Jimmy it reveals.

---

mechanism of a turtle.' – *Beulah Roth*

But of course Jimmy's abiding passion was still for racing fast cars. In an interview shortly before filming on Giant *finished, Jimmy made his racing plans crystal clear.*

'I want to enter at Salinas, Willow Springs, Palm Springs, all the other places. Of course, I'll miss some of them because I have to do a TV spectacular in New York on 18 October. But maybe I can catch a race back there.' – *Jimmy Dean*

'He was a lead foot, hard on engines, but he wasn't afraid of the devil. Even while charging through the pack his face was expressionless. Some drivers frowned, gritted teeth, etc. But not Jimmy. He was totally cool at speed.' – *William Nolan, author*

When asked what Warners thought about his intentions, Jimmy replied:
'When a man goes home at night, the studio

can't tell him what to do.'

With a Lotus Mark 8 already on order from England, Jimmy could not resist buying a silver Porsche Spyder which could reach speeds of 150 mph.

'He was walking with that slow gait of his, a toy monkey on a rubber band hanging from his wrist, hopping up and down with each movement of Jimmy's arm. Jimmy was in a completely carefree, happy mood. We shook hands, and we talked about sports cars, what else? Jimmy wanted to enter the big-car class for cars with the large, powerful engines. That was Jimmy's big dream. And he told me about the big Bristol car he had ordered.

'That was when I remembered about the Porsche Spyder we had on sale. I told Jimmy about this car – told him how powerful it was and that it might be just what he wanted to make his dream come true. It was September 19, 1955. He drove it once around the block. And really liked it. He made one condition before buying the car – he made me promise that I would personally check it before each and every race he took part in, and that I was to ride with him to all the races. Naturally I said ''yes'' because I could think of nothing I'd like better.' – *Rolf Weutherich, car mechanic at Competition Motors*

Jimmy proudly showed off his latest deadly toy round the Giant *set.*
'I turned round and it's James Dean and he motioned for me to step aside. So I excused myself from the group and he said, ''C'mere, I want to show you something.''

'He took me outside the sound stage, and there was this big Porsche sitting there. He told me he'd seen the Porsche and

fallen in love with it and bought it. It was low as a bathtub, and I got in and he took me for a ride around the lot on two wheels. By the time we got back, the sound-stage door opened and everyone else was out there and got all around the Porsche to see Jimmy Dean's new car. It was at this point that I became aware of his psychology. You want everyone to admire your new car, so what do you do? You don't ask your buddy to come out and see it, you shanghai the director – so that there's nothing going on inside and everyone comes outside to see what's happening. Sure enough, he had everyone on the set around him.

'By the time we got back, the studio guards had also come over and said, ''You can never

UN AN APRÈS SA MORT, JIM

Il vérifie sa boîte avant les courses de Palm Springs.

Il vérifie aussi son moteur situé à l'arrière de sa v

Première course : Jimmy se repose en attendant le départ.

L'arbitre donne à James des instructions de dernière minute.

Il est mort il y a un an exactement, en plein succès. Il avait vingt-quatre ans.
Quelques rôles à Broadway, trois grands films et un chagrin d'amour.
La somme de cette courte, ardente et simple vie est tôt faite. Bien plus difficile est d'en comprendre le sens. Et surtout de démêler pourquoi, parmi tant de jeunes morts, c'est celui-ci qu'a choisi la ferveur populaire. Car enfin, ce n'est pas à chaque fois que le cœur innombrable de la foule se fend et prend le deuil. Il n'y a, dans les annales du cinéma, qu'un seul cas analogue : Rudolph Valentino, disparu il y a trente ans et dont le culte demeure vif encore, non seulement dans le souvenir de ceux et celles qui l'ont connu, mais encore dans le mythe né et multiplié après sa mort.
Rudy était lié aux premières grandes scènes d'amour de l'écran et ce sont les femmes, et presque uniquement les femmes, qui l'ont pleuré. Jimmy, bien plus humain et quotidien, bien plus proche de la réalité et des problèmes de son temps, n'exprimait pas seulement l'amour, mais bien plutôt la solitude, le tourment, l'inquiétude et le doute. Ce n'est pas en arrachant les gens à leurs problèmes qu'il les a séduits, mais au contraire en donnant à ces problèmes un visage. Rudy était l'amant du monde, tandis qu'en James Dean, tel revoit un camarade, un frère, un enfant et le

se détruisant et déchirant tout autour de lui jusqu'à rir, drogué, à trente-deux ans...
Ou bien encore Roland Alexandre, Pétrone de scènes et de nos écrans, raffiné et secret, disparat un jour en emportant avec lui son douloureux secr
Ou enfin Robert Francis, que la mort frappa en ciel et qui, se sachant perdu, réussit à piloter son à l'écart de la ville, pour aller s'écraser dans un tière et ne blesser personne.
Et d'autres qu'on a oubliés...
Tandis que, depuis qu'il est mort, James Dean ne de grandir, ni l'attachement de ses innombrables inconnus de s'affirmer. C'est parce que chaque jou courrier nous apporte de plus en plus de demandes co nant sa vie et sa mort que nous avons décidé de répo dans ce numéro à toutes ces questions et de lui adre en cette date anniversaire de sa mort, un témoignage miration, de regret et — il y aurait été par-dessus sensible — de fraternelle et chaude amitié.
Car ce jeune mort que tous, maintenant, pleurent me un ami, a été toute sa vie un solitaire.
Il n'y a pas d'autre mystère ni d'autre drame, ce qui a fait son malheur et, sans doute aussi, l'ess même de son envoûtement.

EST TOUJOURS PARMI NOUS

REPORTAGE GLOBE « EXCLUSIVITE » CINÉMONDE ».

A la fin de sa première course les journalistes se précipitaient afin de l'interviewer. Ce sport dangereux était pour James un stimulant. Chaque fois qu'il avait couru il se montrait souriant.

pour s'intéresser au yogisme ou à la peinture abstraite.
● Les producteurs lui ayant interdit de prendre de trop grands risques tandis qu'il tournait un film, il attendait la fin des prises de vues de *Géant* pour s'inscrire dans la première course d'automne à Salinas. Il y faisait courir sa

● L'autre voiture était conduite par un jeune étudiant de vingt-quatre ans, Donald Turnupseed, qui s'en tira avec quelques plaies sans gravité au visage. Rolf Weutherich eut la mâchoire et un genou brisés. Jimmy avait les deux

quelques semaines avant son accident, il vendit sa moto-cyclette, qu'il menait toujours à un train d'enfer, en expliquant : « C'est vraiment trop dangereux »

After his death, the mythic aspects of Jimmy Dean's character were portrayed through moody photographs which caught the thoughtful side of his nature, as in 'The James Dean Album' (far left), and 'Look' (left).

Jimmy was so fond of the epithet 'Little Bastard' that he had it painted on the side of the Porsche, together with his racing number – 130. He planned to make his return to racing at Salinas in northern California, which was about a seven-hour drive from Los Angeles. But because his Porsche was so new, and had very few miles on the clock, Jimmy decided to drive the car up the Californian coast himself. Another factor in his decision to drive the Porsche himself was that it would allow him to prepare mentally for the race. 'Before I can get in there and drive, I've got to unlimber. I got to be right for it.' *– Jimmy Dean*

So it was that on 30 September 1955 Jimmy sped off with Rolf Weutherich in the passenger seat, and Sanford Roth together with Bill Hickman following behind in a station wagon. Jimmy was in high spirits at the prospect of some serious racing – a luxury he had not been allowed since the Warner crackdown on his racing activities during Rebel Without A Cause. 'I've never seen Jimmy so happy. He talked and laughed and seemed very at ease.' *– Rolf Weutherich*

drive this car on the lot again; you're gonna kill a carpenter or an actor or somebody.'' And that was the last time I saw Jimmy.'
– George Stevens

Ortense and Marcus Winslow were paying a visit to Jimmy and his father at this time.
'He seemed very happy. He showed us the house he had in Sherman Oaks, the big hunting lodge kind of place with just one room. We had dinner with him, and he visited with us out at Winton's house, where we were staying. But we didn't stay too long, because it's a long drive back to Fairmount. He took Marcus for a ride in his Porsche. I didn't want to try it...it's so low.' *– Ortense Winslow*

'In those final days racing was what he cared about most, I had been teaching him things like how to put a car in a four-wheel drift, but he had plenty of skill of his own. If he had lived he might have become a champion driver. We had a running joke. I'd call him 'Little Bastard' and he'd call me 'Big Bastard'. I never stop thinking of those memories.'
– Bill Hickman, stunt driver

The pair laughed and chatted as Jimmy sped along, leaving the station wagon far behind. At 3.30 that afternoon while Jimmy was driving through Bakersfield, he was stopped by a Highway Patrolman and given a speeding ticket for doing 65 mph in a 45 mph zone. His excuse for this transgression of the law:
'I can't get her to run right under eighty.'
– Jimmy Dean

Sandy Roth and Bill Hickman caught up with them, but they agreed to go at their own pace and meet up with each other in Paso Robles. About an hour later Jimmy pulled up at Blackwell's Corner and chatted briefly with another race contestant – Lance Reuson, son of Barbara Hutton. Jimmy complained of his bad luck with the speeding ticket he had just been given.
'And I just done a road safety film. Some fucking journalist is going to love to pick that

up.' - *Jimmy Dean*

Jimmy bought a bag of apples and then was eager to press on with his journey.
'Non-stop to Paso Robles!' – *Jimmy Dean*

At 5.30 the Porsche was speeding along an empty road, with both driver and passenger in a state of semi-tiredness.
'We were not talking now – not of Pier Angeli or of Dean's mother or of anything. The only thought on Jimmy's mind was winning that race. There was no doubt of that; that's all he talked about.' – *Rolf Weutherich*

Up ahead, at the intersection of Routes 466 and 42 in Cholame, a Ford Sedan travelling in the opposite direction started to turn left, having failed to see the silver Porsche plummeting from the south. Jimmy saw the car too late to take any evasive action.
'That guy up there's gotta stop. He's gotta see us.' – *Jimmy Dean*

The two cars hurtled towards each other and crashed. The Porsche crumpled like a matchbox on impact and with it, Jimmy, who was pinned against the steering wheel, his neck broken on impact. Weutherich was thrown clear of the car and the other driver, Donald Turnupseed, was barely injured. Jimmy was pronounced dead on

138

Below: One of the last pictures of Dean, with Rolf
Weutherich, setting off for Salinas in his new Porsche
Spyder – 'the Little Bastard'. Bottom: The wreck of the
Spyder at Cholame.

arrival at hospital and the James Dean legend was
born.

Some have argued that Jimmy's death was inevitable and pre-ordained, that his whole character,
his whole life led up to the point at which he
could achieve immortality by living on after his
death. He certainly had been obsessed with dying
and death from a very early age, possibly because
his mother had died when he was only nine years
old. A friend from the early New York days, Billy
James, remembers:
'Jimmy was *always* interested in death as
a subject. When Jimmy was living at the
Iroquois Hotel, he had a little gallows model
with a light behind it. It was specially lit from
behind so that it projected this huge shadow
on the wall. When you walked into the room,
this huge shadow of a noose was the first
thing you saw.' – *Billy James*

When asked in an interview what he respected
above all else, Jimmy didn't hesitate.
'That's easy. Death. It's the only thing left
to respect. It's the one inevitable, undeniable
truth. Everything else can be questioned. But
death is truth. In it lies the only nobility for
man, and beyond it the only hope.' – *Jimmy
Dean*

The photographer Frank Worth visited Jimmy
at his home the week before the crash, and was
unnerved when he listened to some tapes Jimmy
had been making.
'They gave me the creeps. They were all
about death and dying, poems and things he
just made up. They were his ideas on what it
might be like to die, and how it would feel to
be in the grave and all that.' – *Frank Worth*

Another photographer, Roy Schatt, felt that Jimmy
was on an inexorable path to early death.
'Now the astrologists and numerologists,
those nuts, would say he could see ahead of
his time and all that. *C'mon!* Jimmy was
the kind of guy who you wouldn't bet on the
next moment. Maybe he had a death wish,
but that's a guess. He never told me that. But

he did say, in fact, ''I will not live over thirty.'' And you can play around with that any way you like.' – *Roy Schatt*

In 1955, when Jimmy heard that two Hollywood stars – Bob Travis and Susan Ball – had died, his reply was characteristically sinister.
'Don't worry, I'll be the third.' – *Jimmy Dean*

But his co-star on Rebel Without A Cause, *Natalie Wood, did not feel that Jimmy was unnaturally obsessed with his own mortality.*
'I think he loved life. I think he may have grabbed too strongly at life but I don't think he had a death wish.' – *Natalie Wood*

A great friend, Eartha Kitt, believed Jimmy had a desire to live, to learn and discover, but that often he was thwarted by people who did not understand him.
'He gave off a feeling that is inexplicable. James' popularity went deep into you. And that is what is frightening, and that's why people were saying he's running around on these motorcycles trying to kill himself. Other

people have said to me he's wanting to kill himself, it's what he's after with the racing car, why he's racing the car, but funny...I never thought so at first.

'The person Jamie was looking for within himself he liked. Even though he hadn't gotten to know that person, I think he really and truly did like him and he was very curious, very keen to bring that person to the fore. He liked acting because within it he found all sorts of facades inside of himself, and he was fascinated by them. But actually as far as being interested in the real value of Jamie, I have never found anybody around him that was that interested.

'Maybe they thought they were, but they never actually opened themselves up to get him to come out. If you want to know someone you have to open yourself up in order to bring that person in, to allow that person to exercise what he or she wants.' – *Eartha Kitt*

Jimmy himself was bemused by all the hype surrounding his plans to race fast cars, as he explained to John Gilmore.
'The studio says I'm gonna kill myself, can you figure that? What do you think? I think it's great...doing this article in *Photoplay* and it's got a picture of me sitting on the speedster and it says, ''The studio says this crazy kid's gonna kill himself.'' ' – *Jimmy Dean*

One of the many ironies surrounding Jimmy's death is that the fatal crash was not in the end caused by his fast driving.
'It was impossible for Dean to avoid the crash. Speed was not involved.' – *Policeman at the scene of the crash*

But to many of the Hollywood set – George Stevens among them – the news of Jimmy's death did not come as a complete shock.
'Suddenly the phone rang. I heard him [George Stevens] say, ''No, my God. When? Are you sure?'' And he kind of grunted a

couple of times and hung up the phone. He stopped the film and turned on the lights, stood up and said to the room, ''I've just been given the news that Jimmy Dean has been killed.''

'There was an intake of breath. No one said anything. I couldn't believe it; none of us could. So several of us started calling newspapers, hospitals, police, the morgue. The news was not general at that time. After maybe two hours the word was confirmed.

'Then everybody drifted out to their cars to go home. It was about nine o'clock at night; the studio was deserted. As I walked to my car, feeling numb, I saw a figure coming through the lights down one of the little side-streets. It was George, getting into his Mercedes. We looked at each other, and I said, ''I can't believe it, George. I can't believe it.''

'He said, ''I believe it. He had it coming to him. The way he drove, he had it coming.'' '
– *Elizabeth Taylor*

Inevitably James Dean's death spawned a rash of gushing obituaries (below, from 'The James Dean Album', 1956) ghoulish bandwaggoners (right, as reported in '16 Magazine', 'The James Dean Album', 'Official James Dean Anniversary Book', and 'Jimmy Dean Returns!')

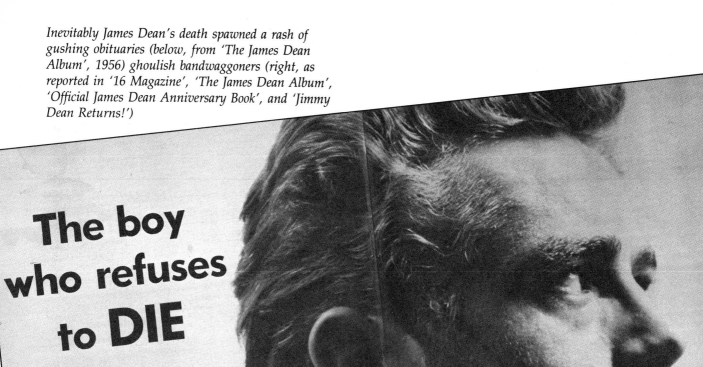

The boy who refuses to DIE

James Dean Lives On . . .

Unforgotten . . . Unforgettable

■ In the months since the life of 24-year-old James Dean was so suddenly snuffed out, an uncanny thing has happened. In the history of Hollywood tragedies, there has never been anything like it. It is almost as if from somewhere in the Great Beyond, with the same intense fire that always burned bright in him, James Dean is defying the fates that took his life before it had really begun, defying them to make him die.

We see it very clearly, now: James Dean is not dead. He is not going to die. We know, because we have the evidence—in many ways. Most poignantly, in the letters and phone calls that are pouring into our office every day. Of course, a certain amount of such interest was to be expected. But, after an interval of mourning, it would normally stop. *It hasn't stopped. And, much more significantly, the people do not speak of Jimmy as if he were dead.*

He is with us, too, when we talk to those who knew him closely, as a friend—and still speak of him as a friend. He is with us in a darkened theater, making the silent place come alive with his vivid brilliance in *East Of Eden*, or *Rebel Without A Cause.* No matter *(Continued on next page)*

As the news filtered around Hollywood, there were many who were deeply saddened and devastated by Jimmy's death.
'James Dean's death had a profound effect on me. The instant I heard about it, I vomited. I don't know why.' – *Montgomery Clift*

People felt that a major talent had been snatched from them before his best had been accomplished.
'His death caused a loss in the movie world that our industry could ill afford. Had he lived long enough I feel he would have made some incredible films; he had sensitivity and a capacity to express emotion.' – *Gary Cooper*

'With his death we lost not only a movie star, but a Hamlet, an Orestes, a Peer Gynt – that is, an actor who could really act.' – *Howard Sackler, playwright*

Only four days after his death, Rebel Without A Cause *was finally released. Reviews of Jimmy's performance as Jim Stark were impressive.*
'Gone are the Brando mannerisms, gone the too-obvious Kazan touch. He stands out as a remarkable talent; and he was cut down

142